Using Informational
Text to Teach
To Kill a Mockingbird

Using Informational
Text to Teach
To Kill a Mockingbird

AUDREY FISCH AND SUSAN CHENELLE

ROWMAN & LITTLEFIELD
Lanham • Boulder • New York • Toronto • Plymouth, UK

Published by Rowman & Littlefield
4501 Forbes Boulevard, Suite 200, Lanham, Maryland 20706
www.rowman.com

10 Thornbury Road, Plymouth PL6 7PP, United Kingdom

British Library Cataloguing in Publication Information Available

Library of Congress Cataloging-in-Publication Data

Fisch, Audrey A.
  Using Informational Text to Teach *To Kill a Mockingbird* / Audrey Fisch and Susan Chenelle.
     pages cm
  ISBN 978-1-4758-0680-9 (pbk. : alk. paper)—ISBN 978-1-4758-0681-6 (electronic)
  1. Lee, Harper. To kill a mockingbird. 2. Lee, Harper—Study and teaching (Secondary)
  I. Chenelle, Susan, 1975– II. Title.
  PS3562.E353T633436 2014
  813'.54—dc23   2014003650

∞™ The paper used in this publication meets the minimum requirements of American National Standard for Information Sciences—Permanence of Paper for Printed Library Materials, ANSI/NISO Z39.48-1992.

Printed in the United States of America

Contents

Two additional units (Unit 8: What Is the Meaning of Rabies in Mockingbird?*: R. A. Craig,* Common Diseases of Farm Animals; *Unit 9: What Does Scout Really Know about Calpurnia?: Claudia Durst Johnson, "Interview: A Perspective on the 1930s") and answers to all sections are available on the series website: www.usinginformationaltext.com.*

Preface

CHANGE

The Common Core Curriculum Standards mean major changes for language arts. English language arts (ELA) teachers are in the process of digesting these changes, particularly the increased emphasis on what the standards call "informational text." Specifically, the Common Core asks language arts teachers to rebalance attention from literature (fiction, drama, and poetry) toward informational texts.

As the standards mandate, students in grade eight should meet a 45 percent literary text/55 percent informational text balance in their reading. Students in grade twelve are expected to achieve a 30 percent literary text/70 percent informational text balance in their reading. These balances include all reading the students will be doing across the grade level in all content areas, not just reading done in ELA classes.

The standards' shift toward informational text has garnered more than a little attention in the media of late. Recently, National Public Radio host Peter Sagal joked that literary classics like *Catcher in the Rye* will soon be replaced by "instructional manuals" like "Executive Order 13423: Strengthening Environmental, Energy, and Transportation Management." The *New York Times*, *Los Angeles Times*, and *Washington Post* have all chimed in, bemoaning what Catherine Gewertz (2012) in *Education Week* called the "literature-pushout."

RESISTANCE

Beyond the media circus, the shift toward informational text, like most changes, has been met with resistance and trepidation on the part of teachers and administrators who do not yet fully understand the requirements of the new standards and how to face the challenges ahead. For many in the field, the changes with regard to informational text are alarming.

Ann Policelli Cronin (2011), writing in *English Leadership Quarterly* (*ELQ*), probably sums up the issues best. She worries that the new standards emphasize "gaining information from texts, not on reading to learn more about oneself, others, and the human condition" (12). She notes, quite rightly, that reading a news story or an inaugural address is different from reading a piece of literature, and she wonders whether the new standards will oversimplify the differences between the "intellectual processes" of these different reading experiences. Cronin articulates a concern that the unique essence of our English classes is somehow going to be lost as we move away from literature. She writes: "The English class is usually the only class in which students are encouraged to grow as interpreters, as questioners, and as divergent and innovative thinkers" (12).

Tom Scott (2011), also writing in *ELQ*, raises many of the same questions, worrying about a lack of attention in the standards to the nature of the "discipline of English" as a part of the humanities and an exclusive focus on the "development of skills with hardly anything said about the value of reading, writing, discussing, and other creative endeavors as means by which we explore and seek to understand human experience" (10). As he explains, speaking for English teachers broadly, "most of us see skills as a means to an end and not as an end in themselves. The value in story, poetry, drama, film, and essay—in reading and producing these texts—lies . . . in the delving into the complexity of what it means to be a human being. . . . These genres can touch our souls" (10).

We agree with Cronin and Scott that English classes should remain unique spaces to develop our students into thinkers with souls. And we agree that literature provides a unique medium through which to foster our students' skills and beings.

Standards' coauthors Susan Pimentel and David Coleman (2012) have tried to respond to the veritable tsunami of resistance; they write in the *Huffington Post* that literature is not "being left by the wayside." Others, like Carol Jago, past president of the National Council of Teachers of English and a member of the Common Core Standards framework committee, have insisted teachers will not have to give up *Romeo and Juliet* and *The Crucible*. As Jago (2013) writes, if that were the case, "I would be up in arms, too."

HOW TO INCORPORATE INFORMATIONAL TEXT WITHOUT THROWING AWAY LITERATURE

So, if the new standards do not ask us to throw away the classics and substitute government position papers and instructional manuals, how are teachers to go about making the meaningful and substantive changes toward nonfiction that the standards require? How do we balance attention toward informational texts without taking away from the teaching of literature (fiction, drama, and poetry)? Sara Mosle (2012), writing in the *New York Times*, suggests that schools need not "more nonfiction but better non-fiction," and she hopes for future anthologies like "30 for Under 20: Great Nonfiction Narratives." While this approach has its appeal, it threatens to further compartmentalize our curriculum and segregate the literary texts we love. As Katie Madsen (2012) writes on an englishcompanion.ning.com forum, "I want the informational texts to relate; otherwise, it feels like stop what we are doing and read this informational piece that doesn't tie into anything." Carol Jago (2013) seems to have Madsen's concerns in mind when she recommends that:

> students compare the lives of the Joads as they left the Dust Bowl to travel west to California in "Grapes of Wrath" with the lives of those who stayed behind through seven years with no rain in Timothy Egan's "The Worst Hard Time" (winner of the 2006 National Book Award for Nonfiction).

Teachers need to be able to incorporate nonfiction in ways that are meaningful, substantive, and enhance rather than taking away from their teaching of literature.

This volume is designed to help you do that work.

HOW THIS VOLUME IS DESIGNED

We have included ten informational texts in nine units, each connected to Harper Lee's *To Kill a Mockingbird*. The informational texts we have selected: (1) are historically specific in their relation to the primary text, (2) provide background to help students contextualize the work, or (3) relate topically or thematically to the primary text. Each informational text, in other words, is deeply connected to the anchor text and will allow your students to strengthen and enrich their analysis of that text.

Each informational text is presented as a part of a unit. The informational text itself is presented in a student-friendly format and annotated with reading strategies for classroom and at-home use. We have secured reproduction permission when possible so that you can copy these articles for use with your students. Using copies (rather than a textbook) allows your students to mark up and annotate the readings, as we would like them to (and as they will be allowed to do on any assessment).

In addition, each unit is built out with extensive vocabulary exercises (meeting the increased emphasis on vocabulary acquisition in the new standards), reading prompts to guide students as they initially work through the informational text, and a variety of discussion and writing prompts, with graphic organizers and scoring rubrics. Most of the open-ended questions ask students to put the informational text into conversation, in one way or another, with *Mockingbird* because we think this is the most valuable element of the new standards and the most important skill we want our students to take away from English class.

For some units, we have also included a more creative group project that allows the students to work collaboratively (anchor standard 1 of the Common Core for speaking and listening) and to present their knowledge and ideas (anchor standards 4, 5, and 6 of the Common Core for speaking and listening) in different formats.

We have also assembled some suggestions for media links that connect with the topics and issues raised in these informational texts. For those of us lucky enough to teach in technology-rich classrooms, these sites offer multimedia connections for our technologically savvy students and visual learners. These sites will allow you to enrich your lessons with brief forays outside the world of text and align your instruction with anchor standard 7 of the Common Core for reading, which calls for students to "integrate and evaluate content presented in diverse media and formats, including visually and quantitatively, as well as in words."

Finally, because we know that teachers are faced with the realities of standardized tests, we have created sets of multiple-choice and open-ended questions you can use with these readings. The multiple-choice questions can be used as assessments, do-nows, exit slips, or in a variety of other ways. Whether we like it or not, multiple-choice questions are a reality in our students' lives, and regular practice at the format of these questions, when based on the material under consideration in class, can make the practice more meaningful and less painful.

All together, then, each unit provides you with a range of choices in a practical, user-friendly format so that you can entice your students into informational readings while helping them annotate, ask questions, draw inferences, synthesize information (including additional research), acquire and own new domain-specific vocabulary, and, most importantly, make connections between the informational text and *Mockingbird*. The latter, after all, is really our goal. We want our students to read, think about, and ultimately love *Mockingbird*, and we hope the readings we have assembled and the activities we have suggested will allow your students to engage with the primary literary text more deeply. In that sense, these informational texts should enrich the experience with the literary text, rather than take our students away from the literature.

Sample answers for all the questions, for your reference, are available on the series website: www.usinginformationaltext.com. The password to open the answer files is mockingbird2014.

WHAT WE HAVE INCLUDED

This volume is not intended to comprise a comprehensive curriculum for teaching *To Kill a Mockingbird*. We have selected a range of readings in different genres and styles (inaugural address, historical analysis, autobiography, etiquette book, farm manual, newspaper editorial, and Supreme Court decision) and on different topics (fear, poverty and entails, proper behavior for a young lady, the right to a lawyer, racial and gender stereotypes, lynching, miscegenation, and heroism). Some of the readings in this volume are historically specific in their relation to the primary text; others provide background to help students contextualize the work; still others relate topically or thematically to the primary text. (Two additional units—an interview with three elderly white women about growing up in the South in the 1930s and an excerpt from a 1915 farm manual about rabies—can be found on the series website at www.usinginformationaltext.com.)

The first set of writing and discussion questions for most units is designed so that students can complete it without any knowledge of *Mockingbird*; that way you can use the reading and some of the activities in the unit as a stand-alone lesson or as a way to build excitement for Harper Lee's novel (a few units require substantial knowledge of the novel and would not work well as stand-alone readings). In general, however, the units are organized in relation to their connection with chapters in *Mockingbird*. Unit 1, on Franklin Delano Roosevelt's first inaugural address, comes first because it connects with Scout's observation, in chapter 1 of *Mockingbird* (1982), that "Maycomb County had recently been told that it had nothing to fear but fear itself" (6). Unit 6, on the Supreme Court's decision in *Loving v. Virginia*, comes near the end because it relates to the character Dolphus Raymond, whom we meet in chapters 16 and 20 of *Mockingbird*.

We do not mean to imply that you should use all of these units any time you teach the novel. We encourage you to read through the units and choose those that fit best with, and will most readily enhance, your approach to the novel. We hope you will find one or more units helpful one year, and then come back and decide to use others the next time you teach the novel. This volume is intended to provide you with the resources that will enrich your instruction of *Mockingbird* in a meaningful and dynamic way for many years to come.

WHY WE WANT TO LEAD THE WAY IN THIS WORK (THAT MANY OF US ARE ALREADY DOING)

As resistance to the Common Core has gained volume and urgency, the Common Core's shift to informational text has been downplayed. Susan Pimentel (2012), for example, lead author of the Common Core State Standards (CCSS) for ELA, writes in the *Huffington Post* of "confusion" about the balance of fiction and nonfiction. She insists that much of the new work with informational text must, as the Common Core State Standards Initiative (2010) suggests, "take place in other classes" since the ELA classroom focuses on literature (5). The big changes, she implies, will be in other classes; language arts teachers do not need to worry.

The larger political battle is likely to rage on for a while as the implementation of the new standards gets underway. Whether or not language arts teachers are going to need to make radical changes or just tinker around the edges of their curriculum, many of us know that the shift toward informational text makes sense because it meets our students' needs. College readiness requires a proficiency in reading informational text. To better prepare our students for the volume and complexity of informational reading that postsecondary education requires, K–12 schools need to adjust. The Common Core emerged out of an understanding of that need. And no amount of discussion about where those needs are going to be met, whether in or out of the language arts classroom, is going to minimize the truth of our students' needs and the reality of our challenge in meeting those needs.

ELA teachers can and should lead the way in incorporating informational text in engaging and meaningful ways in large part because of what the standards (2010) acknowledge to be "the unique, time-honored place of ELA teachers in developing students' literacy skills" (4). This volume was created because we believe that language arts teachers should and can do this work, without taking away from or diminishing what we already do in our ELA classrooms. We want our students to read a range of different texts and to engage with them in a variety of ways. The new standards ask our students to engage in "wide and deep reading of literature and literary nonfiction" in order to "gain a reservoir of literary and cultural knowledge, references, and images; the ability to evaluate intricate arguments; and the capacity to surmount the challenges posed by complex texts" (35). Reading and writing with rigor about fiction and nonfiction: these are the goals of all English teachers.

In *Pathways to the Common Core*, Calkins, Ehrenworth, and Lehman (2012) offer the "exciting thought" that the informational text requirements in the CCSS reading standards have "the potential to take teachers as well as students to new places" (88). As Vicki Otten (2012) writes on the ASCD Express blog, "Content-rich text—both informational and literary—offers numerous opportunities for teaching the reading strategies that will allow students to read, analyze, and write with rigor while relying heavily on the evidence they can pull directly from the text to support their arguments and ideas." In a forum on englishcompanion.ning.com, Susan M. Ulrey (2012) speaks more specifically to the shift toward informational text for offering opportunities to "Motivate [students] to investigate the 'whys' of the events in our ever-changing worlds (worlds is plural for its connotative meanings) . . . [as our students] develop their own thoughts as to where they might take a stand or lend a hand or support as . . . global citizen[s]." Informational texts, in other words, help students make connections between literary works from the past and present-day concerns; the juxtaposition of literary and informational texts enables students to begin to understand and articulate their reactions to the "whys" of the world.

For many of us, then, the standards ask us to make explicit the teaching practices that we have always used: reading and writing about a range of texts. We hope that this book provides resources that will deepen and enrich students' engagements with *Mockingbird* and help teachers align instruction with the Common Core Standards so that our students leave our classrooms better prepared to read, write, think, speak, listen, and collaborate as they face complex issues in our world.

REFERENCES

Calkins, Lucy, Mary Ehrenworth, and Christopher Lehman. *Pathways to the Common Core.* Portsmouth, NH: Heinemann, 2012.

Common Core State Standards Initiative. *Common Core State Standards for English Language Arts and Literacy in History/Social Studies, Science, and Technical Subjects.* Washington, DC, June 2, 2010.

Cronin, Ann P. "Coming to Terms with the Common Core Reading Standards." *English Leadership Quarterly* 34, no. 2 (2011): 11–13.

Gewertz, Catherine. "College and Workplace Demands Are Propelling the Shift in Text." *Education Week*, November 14, 2012. http://www.edweek.org/ew/articles/2012/11/14/12cc -nonfiction.h32.html.

Jago, Carol. "What English Classes Should Look Like in the Common Core Era." *Washington Post*, January 10, 2013. http://www.washingtonpost.com/blogs/answer-sheet/wp/2013/01/10/ what-english-classes-should-look-like-in-common-core-era/.

Lee, Harper. *To Kill a Mockingbird.* New York: Hachette Book Group, 1982.

Madsen, Katie. July 13, 2012 (5:51 p.m.), comment on Katie Madsen, "Informatioanl [*sic*] Texts Database?," *English Companion* (blog), July 11, 2012 (7:04 p.m.), http://englishcompanion .ning.com/group/teachingreadinginmiddleandhighschool/forum/topic/show?groupUrl= teachingreadinginmiddleandhighschool&id=2567740%3ATopic%3A629236&xg_source= msg&groupId=2567740%3AGroup%3A3456&page=2#comments.

Mosle, Sara. "What Should Children Read?" *New York Times*, November 22, 2012. http:// opinionator.blogs.nytimes.com/2012/11/22/what-should-children-read/.

Otten, Vicki. "A Common Implementation Manifesto." *ASCD*, July 19, 2012. http://www.ascd .org/ascd-express/vol7/721–newvoices.aspx (accessed August 20, 2012).

Pimentel, Susan, and David Coleman. "The Role of Fiction in the High School Language Arts Classroom." *Huffington Post*, December 11, 2012. http://www.huffingtonpost.com/susan -pimentel/the-role-of-fiction-in-th_b_2279782.html.

Sagal, Peter. "Wait Wait . . . Don't Tell Me Panel Round Two." *Wait Wait . . . Don't Tell Me.* Prod. WBEZ. Chicago, IL, December 15, 2012.

Scott, Tom. "CEL Member Profile: Tom Scott." *English Leadership Quarterly* 34, no. 2 (2011): 10–11.

Ulrey, Susan M. *Re: Common Core: It's Complexical.* March 11, 2012. http://englishcompanion .ning.com/profiles/blog/show?id=2567740:BlogPost:596521 (accessed August 20, 2012).

How to Use This Book

This book is designed to make it easy for you to include informational text in coordination with your teaching of your primary literary text.

THE INFORMATIONAL TEXTS

We have included a wide range of materials, in terms of reading level, subject matter, and style of writing. Some materials are historical in orientation and offer background information; others are more polemical in nature and offer students a window into controversies about the text; others are simply unusual, dynamic pieces that we think offer students different reading experiences as well interesting connections with *Mockingbird*.

Read through the texts. Which will best fit your existing emphasis with *Mockingbird*? Which will enable you to fill in gaps in your students' knowledge or understanding of the text? Which will help your students be excited about and connect with Harper Lee's novel?

The answers to these questions will, and should, change year after year. Each year, balance your personal taste with the needs of your students and select different informational texts to incorporate into your teaching!

TEACHER'S GUIDE

Each section begins with a brief teacher's guide, in which we address the challenges and possibilities offered by the featured informational text. The teacher's guide also indicates which suggested rubric (see below) should be used with the writing activities and whether the writing and discussion activities require any additional research on the part of the students.

The teacher's guide also includes suggested timing for how and when the informational text and the related discussion and writing activities can be integrated into your teaching of *Mockingbird*. Nearly all of the informational texts can be read without any knowledge of Lee's text. You may choose, for example, to begin your unit on *Mockingbird* with *Loving v. Virginia*. You will find activities to support that timing and that require no prior knowledge of the novel but will also pique your students' interest. Other activities in each unit, however, are better timed at particular moments in your students' reading process, so you might, for example, return to some of the activities in the *Loving* unit when you reach the relevant chapters about Dolphus Raymond in *Mockingbird*.

ESSENTIAL QUESTIONS

Each article and each writing activity begins with an essential question to guide students' study of the featured informational text. Following Grant Wiggins' backward-design model (2005, 110), we have designed the questions for each article to enable teachers not to assess student understanding or "coverage" of the article, but instead to

1. create authentic inquiry into big ideas
2. provoke sustained thought and investigation
3. require the use of evidence and the consideration of alternate viewpoints
4. promote rethinking of assumptions
5. produce connections with personal experience and prior learning
6. allow for the meaningful transfer of reading, thinking, speaking, listening, and writing skills.[1]

Our essential questions are designed, in other words, to create pathways into the informational texts and suggest connections between each informational text and *Mockingbird*.

Of course, many other pathways and connections exist, and we hope you will use this text to get your students comfortable with the idea of creating their own essential questions, driven by their interests and concerns.

MEDIA LINKS

Within the teacher's guide that accompanies each section, we have included a list of media links that connect with the topics and issues raised in these informational texts. These resources include online video and audio clips, full-length documentaries, and multimedia slideshows. In this list, we have provided enough descriptive detail about each resource (rather than listing specific URLs, since web page addresses change so frequently) that you should be able to find it through any Internet search engine.

We encourage you to use these resources not just to build background knowledge for the informational texts and *Mockingbird*, but to use the media resources in dialogue with the novel, with the informational texts in this book and with each other, so that students can "integrate and evaluate content presented in diverse media and formats, including visually and quantitatively, as well as in words," as called for by the CCSS reading anchor standard 7. These media resources also offer a meaningful way, as Sarah Brown Wessling notes (2011, 44) to "meet our learners where they are: at the screen" and "alter their habits" as viewers in order to alter their habits as readers. In doing so we can help our students draw out layers of meaning from these texts and "recognize and employ the kind of complex process that feeds all facets of literacy: reading, writing, speaking, language, *and* viewing" (47).

VOCABULARY AND THE NEW LANGUAGE STANDARD

Reading informational text poses new challenges for our students in terms of both academic and domain-specific vocabulary, and the new Common Core language standard places increased emphasis on addressing these challenges. We have designed a range of activities to help you meet your students' needs, to make the informational texts accessible, and to take advantage of the opportunities these texts provide for enhanced vocabulary acquisition and use.

We begin each section with a vocabulary warm-up, which precedes the article and will facilitate understanding of challenging vocabulary prior to reading the text. We have crafted these activities not only to front load challenging vocabulary but to introduce concepts students will encounter in the article as well. Discussion of these words in conjunction with the section's essential question can help promote students' interest in reading the article, encourage them to ask their own prereading questions, and support their confidence in comprehending the article.

The vocabulary questions are constructed in a variety of ways to meet the needs of the new language standard. Sections A and B address anchor standard 4 for language, asking students to develop their ability to use context clues to determine the meaning of words in multiple choice and open-ended-style questions. Section C asks students to deepen their knowledge and critical approach to language by learning to practice their dictionary skills (anchor standard 4 for language) in relation to words that appear to be common but are used in uncommon, unfamiliar ways. Section D asks students again to use dictionaries to determine the meaning of a word but is designed to promote authentic and engaging use of the word by the student. Section E involves students using the words in different forms or with different endings, again to promote extensive and useful practice. Section F gives students the opportunity to solidify their ownership of the vocabulary by using them in original skits. The vocabulary skits are intended to create "massive practice" (Moffett and Wagner 1991, 10), so that your students work extensively with the new words in ways that are both fun and meaningful.

This combination of exercises is intended to offer multiple opportunities for students to practice the vocabulary acquisition skills listed in the Common Core State Standards (CCSS), based on the model for "rich" vocabulary instruction that moves "beyond definitional information" and works "to get students actively involved in using and thinking about word meanings and creating lots of associations among words" as outlined by Beck, McKeown, and Kucan (2002, 73).

The vocabulary warm-up questions can be used in any number of ways. Students can complete all the questions individually in class or as homework. However, group work, whether in class or outside class, in which groups of students are assigned sets of questions that they answer and then teach to their peers can be a more efficient use of class time. We strongly advocate continued and explicit attention to the use of these vocabulary words in class and in future writing.

In addition, vocabulary-related questions recur in the sidebars alongside the articles as readers are asked to use their vocabulary knowledge to translate the pieces of the informational text into their own words. Follow-up vocabulary questions are included in the "Check for Understanding" section after each article to assess student comprehension of key vocabulary words as well as their ability to apply the vocabulary acquisition skills addressed in the warm-up section.

THE INFORMATIONAL READINGS

Each informational text is presented to your students with a number of features.

First, we created a brief introduction to each reading, in which students can learn a bit about the text they are going to read.

Second, we have marked up (and in some cases edited down) the informational text, highlighting key moments in the reading (and eliminating extraneous or distracting information).

Third, we have created sidebars for use by students or teachers in working through the informational text. The sidebars ask students to reflect on the essential question, on the introduction, and on key ideas throughout the reading. They ask students to put key concepts and phrases with difficult vocabulary into their own words. And they call students' attention to important moments or concepts in the reading. The sidebars, then, offer guidance, helping the students to "chunk" and negotiate what might otherwise be a difficult or overwhelming text. We hope the strategies we offer will also teach students generally how they might approach and work through challenging texts.

PHOTOCOPYING

We have secured reproduction permission when possible so that you can copy these articles for use with your students. This allows you and your students to take full advantage of the reading features. Encourage your students to further mark up and annotate the copies as they read.

DISCUSSION AND WRITING

For each article, we have created a range of discussion and writing activities. The relevant Common Core Standards (we have used the standards for grades nine through ten as our baseline, so you will need to tinker with our standards if you are using *Mockingbird* in another grade) are listed at the beginning of each activity. Our questions address a range of the requirements of the CCSS, including discussion and writing activities that focus on key ideas and details, craft and structure, as well as integration of knowledge and ideas. Most units contain at least one question that requires students to gather relevant research and synthesize multiple sources, meeting the anchor writing standard, "Research to Build and Present Knowledge." In addition, every question makes explicit which standards it addresses, allowing you as the teacher to know how you are meeting the needs of the CCSS and allowing your students to see what your expectations for them are.

It is not likely that you will have the time or inclination to undertake all the suggested questions. Instead, pick and choose as serves your purposes. Or allow your students to choose the tasks that most interest them. Each activity begins with a preliminary discussion question or questions that can be used as do-nows, in small-group or whole-class discussion, or as homework before undertaking the larger writing tasks. Feel free as well to use some of these discussion questions as classroom activities without going on to ask your students to complete the follow-up writing task.

Also, whenever possible, we have included simple graphic organizers to help students prepare to write by assembling and organizing their evidence beforehand. In general, the organizer models the work for students, using examples to show how the organizer is to be completed. Feel free to use these organizers as much or as little as your students find helpful. We have attempted to format them so that you can just photocopy them directly from the book, but you can download them from www.usinginformationaltext .com in a format that you can modify if necessary, particularly as you differentiate your instruction for all the learners in your classroom.

You can indicate and vary the expectations of the length of student responses for each prompt. We imagine an average length of one to two pages for each writing task, although some prompts obviously lend themselves to longer responses than others. With each writing task, we explicitly call for the use of textual evidence in order to meet the increased emphasis on using evidence in the writing standard. Still, your expectations will vary based on the time allocated, the depth of your interest in and discussion of the reading, and the needs of your students.

In addition, we have arranged the various exercises and activities to try to minimize the required copying. Whenever possible, each discussion and writing task and any accompanying graphic organizers will fit on one double-sided page, so that your students will have their prewriting and discussion notes and materials at the ready when they attack the writing prompt.

RUBRICS

For each writing prompt, we suggest in the teacher's guide one of two provided rubrics that can be found at the end of the volume (coded by letter, one for writing that requires research and one for writing that does not require research). Rubrics for the class activities are highly specific and are included immediately following those assignments within the unit.

The rubrics are intended to help you communicate expectations to your students and incorporate the language and requirements of the CCSS. Of course, you should feel free to adapt these rubrics to your own priorities and your students' needs or to use your own rubric entirely. Should you choose to use ours, you can also develop your own grading criteria to correlate with the point structure of the rubric (15–16 points = A–, for example) or use the rubrics holistically. These rubrics are available at www.usinginformationaltext.com in formats that you can modify as you wish.

Note that for each rubric, we have included criteria for vocabulary and for documentation accuracy (in-text citation and works cited), so that these skills are reinforced regularly, as per the new language standard.

We encourage you, when undertaking any of the writing prompts, to share the rubric and review the criteria at the top of the rubric page at the time you introduce the assignment, so that students are aware of your expectations from the beginning. Rubrics also offer a valuable opportunity for the students to peer and self-evaluate as they are revising and upon completion of the task.

CLASS ACTIVITIES

In addition to the writing and discussion activities, we have included for some of the informational texts a class-wide or small-group project that asks the students to work collaboratively (anchor standard 1 of the Common Core for speaking and listening) and to present their knowledge and ideas (anchor standards 4, 5, and 6 of the Common Core for speaking and listening) in different kinds of formats. These projects are ideal for differentiating instruction and ask students to apply their understanding of the informational text and the novel in creative ways. Ranging from conducting a TV talk show debate to producing a video news report—the projects draw on and develop diverse learning styles as well as students' abilities to use "strong content knowledge" and evidence to demonstrate not only comprehension but critique and understanding of diverse perspectives, which the CCSS identifies as necessary for college and career readiness (2010, 7).

In order to forestall some of the difficulties of assessing creative and group projects, each project requires a narrative explanation, in which the students must explain the goals and choices of the group and how the end product responds to the requirements of the assignment. Students are also required to write a narrative in which they evaluate their group's collaborative process and their own roles in the group.

While most of the projects we have suggested would be most appropriate to undertake after students have finished or nearly finished reading the novel, feel free to adapt the scope and requirements of each project according to available time and students' needs and interests. For each project, we have supplied a sample rubric that incorporates the relevant language and requirements of the CCSS for each project as well.

ANSWERS

Answers and sample responses to the questions in each unit are available on the series website: www.usinginformationaltext.com. The password to open the answer file is mockingbird2014. We provide an answer key containing sample correct responses for all multiple choice questions as well as brief suggestions for the different constructed responses. Our completed organizers and sample responses are not intended to serve as models for student use but to work as brief, suggestive, and by no means comprehensive guidelines for teacher use only. The responses are not the only correct answers, and student responses should not be considered incorrect if they do not conform exactly to what we have offered.

WEBSITE

On our website (www.usinginformationaltext.com), you will find two additional units (an interview with three elderly white women about growing up in the South in the 1930s and an excerpt from a 1915 farm manual about rabies) along with updated resources—new articles, activities, and media links. You can also download any of the graphic organizers and rubrics to be edited and modified as you need. We hope you will also share feedback and ideas on our teacher blog.

ENJOY

The CCSS set a high bar for language arts teachers. Expectations, however, without sufficient resources and professional development do not ensure positive or effective change. We know language arts teachers are busy professionals with a host of responsibilities both in and outside the classroom. We hope that the resources we have assembled here will make it easier for you to adjust and adapt to the new standards while reinvigorating your teaching and your students' engagement with *Mockingbird*. Mostly, we hope they will allow you to make your language arts classroom a place for you and your students to have fun while learning.

NOTE

1. Modified from Grant Wiggins and Jay McTighe, *Understanding by Design* (Upper Saddle River, NJ: Pearson, 2005), 110.

REFERENCES

Beck, Isabel L., Margaret G. McKeown, and Linda Kucan. *Bringing Words to Life*. New York: Guilford, 2002.

Common Core State Standards Initiative. *Common Core State Standards for English Language Arts and Literacy in History/Social Studies, Science, and Technical Subjects*. Washington, DC: Common Core State Standards Initiative, 2010.

Moffett, James, and Betty J. Wagner. *Student-Centered Language Arts, K–12*. New York: Heinemann, 1991.

Wessling, Sarah Brown, Danielle Lillge, and Crystal VanKooten. *Supporting Students in a Time of Core Standards: English Language Arts, Grades 9–12*. Urbana, IL: National Council of Teachers of English, 2011.

Wiggins, Grant, and Jay McTighe. *Understanding by Design*. Upper Saddle River, NJ: Pearson, 2005.

What Do Americans Have to Fear?

Franklin Delano Roosevelt, "The Only Thing We Have to Fear Is Fear Itself"

TEACHER'S GUIDE
Overview

Harper Lee alludes to Roosevelt's first inaugural address and its most famous phrase as she introduces readers to the world of Maycomb, so students will benefit from some understanding of the challenges facing the nation in the 1930s. More broadly, discussion of the address will allow students the opportunity to consider key ideas in Roosevelt's speech regarding good neighbors, interdependence, and democracy and to consider how these same themes permeate *Mockingbird*.

Timing

This excerpt is best used early on, before students have begun *Mockingbird* or as students are reading through the first few chapters and learning about the community and setting of the novel. The excerpt can also be used fruitfully in relation to chapter 26, when Miss Gates discusses Hitler with the children in school.

Consider the following guidelines regarding when to undertake the different activities:

Essential question for discussion and writing	Objective	Suggested timing	Suggested rubric	Additional research
A. How does Roosevelt craft his speech?	Students will (SW) analyze Roosevelt's use of language in order to write an essay evaluating its effect on his listeners (or readers today).	any time—this set of questions doesn't require any knowledge of *Mockingbird*	A	N
B. Afraid or not?	SW analyze the theme of fear in both the address and *Mockingbird* in order to write an essay evaluating whether the residents of Maycomb County seem optimistic or fearful.	after chapter 3 (when Scout begins school)	A	N
C. Should we have faith in democracy?	SW analyze the concept and reality of democracy in order to write an essay comparing Lee's and Roosevelt's views on American democracy.	after chapter 26 (when Miss Gates discusses Hitler with the children)	B	Y
D. What is a good neighbor?	SW analyze the "policy of the good neighbor" in order to write an essay evaluating how Lee's characters exemplify this policy or not.	after students have completed the novel, but could be used earlier in a limited way	A	N
E. What does it mean to be interdependent?	SW analyze the theme of interdependence in both Roosevelt's address and in *Mockingbird* in order to write an essay evaluating how Lee's characters embrace or reject interdependence with others.	after students have completed the novel, but could be used earlier in a limited way	A	N
Class Activity				
Reporting on the "Inaugural"	SW select parts of Roosevelt's speech and conduct interviews in order to produce and present a multimedia news report on Roosevelt's inauguration.	after chapter 3 or any time later (when Scout begins school and students have sufficient basic knowledge of the cast of characters in the novel)	rubric included	Y

Notes on the Article

- Students may benefit from some background information on the Depression, but teachers should not feel forced to turn this into a history lesson. As Roosevelt (and Lee) make clear, the 1930s was a time of economic distress and uncertainty.

- The first two paragraphs of the address are engaging as both political rhetoric and theater. Students might benefit from some dramatic oral performances of these paragraphs.

- We have omitted sections of the address that discuss specific problems in the credit market; we have also omitted sections where Roosevelt asks for swift Congressional cooperation and extended executive authority. Both of these seem outside the scope of the address at least as it relates to *Mockingbird*.

- Key vocabulary: inaugural, candor, curtailment, temper, arduous, values, impel, optimist, languishes, unscrupulous, evanescent

Suggested Media Links

- PBS's *American Experience: The 1930s*—DVD collection and clips available online
- PBS's *The Great Depression: Stories of a Generation's Struggle for Democracy*—DVD and clips available online
- New York Times *Web Special: The Crash of 1929*
- Online audio of "Brother Can You Spare a Dime"—YouTube version available performed by Bing Crosby with great visuals
- Online video of Roosevelt's swearing-in and inaugural address—available on YouTube
- Recording of interviews with Hattie Adolphus and Ruth Brunner on how the Depression affected their families, including their views on Franklin and Eleanor Roosevelt—available online in the University of Alabama digital archives

VOCABULARY WARM-UP

L.9-10.4, L.9-10.5, L.9-10.6

> **Words to own:** inaugural, candor, curtailment, temper, arduous, values, impel, optimist, languishes, unscrupulous, evanescent

Section A: Use context clues. Read the following sentences and use context clues to determine the meaning of the italicized words.

1. President Franklin Delano Roosevelt delivered his first *inaugural* address after taking the oath of office. Based on the context here, what is an *inaugural* address? What does it mean to be *inaugurated*?

2. Roosevelt writes of a crisis based on the fact that government "is faced by a serious *curtailment* of income." Based on the context in which it is used, what do you think a *curtailment* of income means? Does the government have more or less money than previously? Why?

3. Roosevelt seeks to balance his pessimistic view of "*arduous* days that lie before us" with his *optimistic* view of "the warm courage of national unity." Based on the context here, you can infer that *arduous* means what?

4. Roosevelt argues that "plenty is at our doorstep, but a generous use of it *languishes* in the very sight of the supply." If our use of the plenty we have *languishes* as a result of seeing the large supplies we have, is Roosevelt suggesting that we are using our plenty fully or not?

Section B: More context clues. Here your task is to use context clues to understand the word's meaning and to practice your context clues skills.

1. Happiness can be *evanescent*; a moment later, you think of something sad and your mood changes. *Evanescent* here means
   a) long-lasting
   b) short-lived
   c) sad
   d) eventual

2. Which word from the sentence in question 1 best helps the reader understand the meaning of *evanescent*?
   a) moment
   b) sad
   c) later
   d) happiness

3. Democracy can *languish* if the population is apathetic and indifferent; if we want our system of government to remain strong, we need to be involved and engaged. *Languish* here means
   a) weaken
   b) strengthen
   c) linger
   d) improve

4. Which word from the sentence in question 3 best helps the reader understand the meaning of *languish*?
   a) population
   b) system
   c) strong
   d) democracy

Section C: Use the dictionary in order to understand the uncommon meanings of these common words.

1. "*Values* have shrunken to fantastic levels; taxes have risen." Here, Roosevelt uses the term *values* to refer not to morals and ethics but to what?

2. Roosevelt references his ability to "read the *temper* of our people." He does not mean the level of anger of our people. What does he mean by *temper*?

Section D: Use the dictionary to look up the italicized words and answer the following questions based on their definitions.

1. Do you expect *candor* from your friends? Why or why not?

2. Your mother may want to *impel* you to get good grades, but only you can master your own success? Why?

May be photocopied for classroom use. *Using Informational Text to Teach* To Kill a Mockingbird by Audrey Fisch and Susan Chenelle © 2014 (Lanham, MD: Rowman & Littlefield).

3. Would you expect schoolwork to be *arduous*? Why or why not?

4. If you say that your father is an *optimistic* person, what do you mean?

5. If a politician is *unscrupulous*, what sorts of things might he or she do? Why?

6. If a business has *evanescent* profits, would you expect it to be around for a long time? Why or why not?

Section E: Practice using the word correctly by choosing the correct form of the word that best fits in the blank within the following sentences.

1. Although my friend generally speaks with honesty and _____, she is reluctant to tell her mother that she doesn't like her cooking.
   a) candor
   b) candidly
   c) candid
   d) candors

2. Some people are self-motivated; I am one of them; my desire to improve my skills is what _____ me to practice and practice.
   a) impel
   b) impels
   c) impelled
   d) impelling

3. Some politicians think that if we _____ government spending, we will be able to stimulate more private sector investment and growth generally in the economy.
   a) curtailment
   b) curtails
   c) curtailed
   d) curtail

4. My sister is always looking on the bright side; she is an eternal _____.
   a) optimistic
   b) optimist
   c) optimists
   d) optimistically

Section F: Vocabulary skits. Use the model sentences and definitions to understand the words in question. Create a skit in which you address the given topic. Every member of the group must use the vocabulary word at least once during your performance of the skit.

1. *candor*—openness, truthfulness, sincerity
   - He spoke with *candor* about painful incidents from his past that another man might have tried to hide.
   - Teenagers sometimes don't speak *candidly* with their parents about what is really going on in their lives because they don't want their parents to know!
   - Susan was praised by some for her *candor*, but others found her to be blunt, too honest, and therefore rude in always telling the truth.

Scenario: Create a skit in which some teenagers discuss whether or not to be *candid* with their parents about what went on at a party. Some feel *candor* is best; others feel complete *candor* is unnecessary.

2. *optimist*—somebody positive and hopeful about the future
   - My sister is always an *optimist*; if she gets a bad grade in school, she always holds out hope that the teacher miscalculated the grade and that she might have earned a better mark.
   - I sometimes find it difficult to be *optimistic* about our troubled, dangerous, beleaguered world.
   - Do you always see the cup as half full? Then you are an *optimist*.

Scenario: Create a skit in which a small group is shipwrecked on a desert island. There is no food, no water, no supplies, and no hope. One in the group, however, remains *optimistic* to the dismay and disbelief of his or her companions.

3. *arduous*—difficult, tiring, demanding, tough
   - The work may be *arduous*, but nothing valuable was ever easy.
   - The educational journey toward becoming a doctor is *arduous*, but the ability to help people in times of great need is a tremendous reward.
   - I find our football practices to be *arduous* and dull, but the coach says practice is meant to be tough.

Scenario: Create a skit in which some young employees ask for a raise at their place of business based on the fact that the work required is particularly *arduous*.

---

4. *impel*—force to do something, cause to move
  - The government's unfair policies *impelled* young people all over the country to protest.
  - Congress was *impelled* to change the law because of the outpouring of letters from citizens.
  - You cannot *impel* me to change my mind; your arguments are ineffective, and my decision is made.

Scenario: Create a skit in which a group of students complains to the school principal about the school food. The students need to *impel* the principal to take action, but he is reluctant.

ESSENTIAL QUESTION: WHAT DO AMERICANS HAVE TO FEAR?
Introduction

In his first *inaugural* address (1933), Franklin Delano Roosevelt (1882–1945), the thirty-second president of the United States, took on the issues facing the nation at the height of the Depression. Lee alludes to President Roosevelt's address in the first chapter of *Mockingbird* when she writes, "it was a time of vague optimism . . . Maycomb County had recently been told that it had nothing to fear but fear itself."

Reflect on the essential question: What does the question suggest to you? What do you think Americans fear today? What do you think the article will be about?

Reflect on the introduction: The introduction tells you that the piece you are about to read was Roosevelt's first inaugural address. What does that mean about the occasion when Roosevelt delivered his comments? How do you think the time (1933) and context (the Depression) influenced what he said?

Reflect on the title: "The Only Thing We Have to Fear Is Fear Itself." Have you heard this phrase before? What does it mean to you?

"The Only Thing We Have to Fear Is Fear Itself": FDR's First Inaugural Address
By Franklin D. Roosevelt

I am certain that my fellow Americans expect that on my induction into the Presidency I will address them with a *candor* and a decision which the present situation of our people *impel*. This is preeminently the time to speak the truth, the whole truth, frankly and boldly. Nor need we shrink from honestly facing conditions in our country today. This great Nation will endure as it has endured, will revive and will prosper. So, first of all, let me assert my firm belief that the only thing we have to fear is fear itself— nameless, unreasoning, unjustified terror which paralyzes needed efforts to convert retreat into advance. In every dark hour of our national life a leadership of frankness and vigor has met with that understanding and support of the people themselves which is essential to victory. I am convinced that you will again give that support to leadership in these critical days.

In such a spirit on my part and on yours we face our common difficulties. They concern, thank God, only material things. *Values*

Vocabulary: Roosevelt says he will address the American people "with a candor and a decision which the present situation of our people impel." Put this into your own words.

Notice that Roosevelt includes in his speech here the words that form his title. Why do you think he does that? What is particularly important about these words? Do you have a greater understanding now about what fears Americans in the 1930s were facing?

---

have shrunken to fantastic levels; taxes have risen; our ability to pay has fallen; government of all kinds is faced by serious *curtailment* of income; the means of exchange are frozen in the currents of trade; the withered leaves of industrial enterprise lie on every side; farmers find no markets for their produce; the savings of many years in thousands of families are gone.

> **Vocabulary**: Roosevelt says that "Values have shrunken to fantastic levels." He isn't talking about social or moral values. What is he saying? Put this into your own words.
>
> **Notice** the image here: "the means of exchange are frozen in the currents of trade." Do we typically describe trade in terms of currents or in terms of being frozen? What is Roosevelt doing with his language here?
>
> **Vocabulary**: Roosevelt says that "only a foolish optimist can deny the dark realities of the moment." What is he saying? Put this into your own words.

More important, a host of unemployed citizens face the grim problem of existence, and an equally great number toil with little return. Only a foolish *optimist* can deny the dark realities of the moment.

Yet our distress comes from no failure of substance. We are stricken by no plague of locusts. Compared with the perils which our forefathers conquered because they believed and were not afraid, we have still much to be thankful for. Nature still offers her bounty and human efforts have multiplied it. Plenty is at our doorstep, but a generous use of it *languishes* in the very sight of the supply. Primarily this is because the rulers of the exchange of mankind's goods have failed, through their own stubbornness and their own incompetence, have admitted their failure, and abdicated. Practices of the *unscrupulous* money changers stand indicted in the court of public opinion, rejected by the hearts and minds of men.

[Here, Roosevelt turns to specific criticism of the credit market.]

Happiness lies not in the mere possession of money; it lies in the joy of achievement, in the thrill of creative effort. The joy and moral stimulation of work no longer must be forgotten in the mad chase of *evanescent* profits. These dark days will be worth all they cost us if they teach us that our true destiny is not to be ministered unto but to minister to ourselves and to our fellow men.

[Next, Roosevelt addresses how he plans to restore public confidence.]

This Nation asks for action, and action now.

Our greatest primary task is to put people to work. This is no

> **Key idea**: Roosevelt references "our true destiny." What do you think he means by this phrase? How is our true destiny different from "the mad chase of evanescent profits"?
>
> **Key idea**: Roosevelt is comparing unemployment with war. Why? What is his proposal for solving unemployment?

unsolvable problem if we face it wisely and courageously. It can be accomplished in part by direct recruiting by the Government itself, treating the task as we would treat the emergency of a war, but at the same time, through this employment, accomplishing greatly needed projects to stimulate and reorganize the use of our natural resources.

Hand in hand with this we must frankly recognize the overbalance of population in our industrial centers and, by engaging on a national scale in a redistribution, endeavor to provide a better use of the land for those best fitted for the land. The task can be helped by definite efforts to raise the values of agricultural products and with this the power to purchase the output of our cities. It can be helped by preventing realistically the tragedy of the growing loss through foreclosure of our small homes and our farms. It can be helped by insistence that the Federal, State, and local governments act forthwith on the demand that their cost be drastically reduced. It can be helped by the unifying of relief activities which today are often scattered, uneconomical, and unequal. It can be helped by national planning for and supervision of all forms of transportation and of communications and other utilities which have a definitely public character. There are many ways in which it can be helped, but it can never be helped merely by talking about it. We must act and act quickly.

[Here Roosevelt offers some specifics regarding banking reform.]

The basic thought that guides these specific means of national recovery is not narrowly nationalistic. It is the insistence, as a first consideration, upon the interdependence of the various elements in all parts of the United States—a recognition of the old and permanently important manifestation of the American spirit of the pioneer. It is the way to recovery. It is the immediate way. It is the strongest assurance that the recovery will endure.

In the field of world policy I would dedicate this Nation to the policy of the good neighbor—the neighbor who resolutely respects himself and, because he does so, respects the rights of others—the neighbor who respects his obligations and respects the sanctity of his agreements in and with a world of neighbors.

If I read the *temper* of our people correctly, we now realize as we have never realized before our interdependence on each other; that we can not merely take but we

> **Key idea:** Roosevelt articulates here his "policy of the good neighbor." What do you think he means by this? What does he see as good neighborliness?
>
> **Key idea:** Roosevelt suggests that we may not before have realized "our interdependence on each other." How do you think he sees the troubles the nation faces as the result of a lack of recognition of our interdependence? How will recognition of our interdependence make us stronger as a nation? What changes, including those mentioned in the speech, reflect an understanding of our interdependence? Why?

must give as well; that if we are to go forward, we must move as a trained and loyal army willing to sacrifice for the good of a common discipline, because without such discipline no progress is made, no leadership becomes effective. We are, I know, ready and willing to submit our lives and property to such discipline, because it makes possible a leadership which aims at a larger good. This I propose to offer, pledging that the larger purposes will bind upon us all as a sacred obligation with a unity of duty hitherto evoked only in time of armed strife.

With this pledge taken, I assume unhesitatingly the leadership of this great army of our people dedicated to a disciplined attack upon our common problems.

[*Roosevelt asks for the cooperation of Congress and an expansion of his executive powers.*]

For the trust reposed in me I will return the courage and the devotion that befit the time. I can do no less.

We face the *arduous* days that lie before us in the warm courage of the national unity; with the clear consciousness of seeking old and precious moral *values*; with the clean satisfaction that comes from the stern performance of duty by old and young alike. We aim at the assurance of a rounded and permanent national life.

We do not distrust the future of essential democracy. The people of the United States have not failed. In their need they have registered a mandate that they want direct, vigorous action. They have asked for discipline and direction under leadership. They have made me the present instrument of their wishes. In the spirit of the gift I take it.

Key idea: Why do you think Roosevelt brings up democracy here, toward the end of his speech? Why does he call it essential?

Consider the last three sentences of Roosevelt's speech. What do you notice? How is he trying to appeal to the American people? In what ways is he trying to promote his ideas for change?

Vocabulary: Roosevelt says that "We face arduous days that lie before us in the warm courage of the national unity." What do you understand him to mean by arduous days? What do you think it means to describe courage as warm? Put Roosevelt's sentence into your own words.

In this dedication of a Nation we humbly ask the blessing of God. May He protect each and every one of us. May He guide me in the days to come.

Roosevelt, Franklin D. "First Inaugural Address." 1933 Presidential Inauguration. U.S. Capitol, Washington, DC. 4 Mar. 1933. Address.

CHECK FOR UNDERSTANDING

RL.9-10.4, RI.9-10.1, RI.9-10.4, RI.9-10.6, RI.9-10.9

1. Roosevelt writes: "*Values* have shrunken to fantastic levels; taxes have risen; our ability to pay has fallen." By *values*, he likely means
   a) social norms
   b) morals
   c) ethics
   d) monetary worth

2. Roosevelt writes: "Only a foolish *optimist* can deny the dark realities of the moment." By *optimist*, he means a(n)
   a) fool
   b) realist
   c) idealist
   d) racist

3. Harper Lee's invocation of Roosevelt's inaugural address in *To Kill a Mockingbird* is an example of
   a) an allusion
   b) a metaphor
   c) plagiarism
   d) point of view

4. Roosevelt's main goal in his inaugural address seems to be
   a) to outline the problems the country is suffering under because of the Depression.
   b) to blame Congress for not acting earlier to resolve the issues.
   c) to inspire the nation with optimism.
   d) to inspire the nation with optimism about his proposal for reform.

5. Toward the end of the address, Roosevelt writes: "They have made me the present instrument of their wishes." By this statement, he is trying to assert
   a) that his policies represent the wishes of the people.
   b) that the people wish he would be instrumental.
   c) that he can solve the problems the country faces.
   d) that his leadership is instrumental.

WRITING AND DISCUSSION

RI.9-10.1, RI.9-10.4, RI.9-10.5, RI.9-10.6, RI.9-10.9, W.9-10.2, W.9-10.4, W.9-10.5, W.9-10.9, SL.9-10.1, SL.9-10.3, L.9-10.1, L.9-10.2, L.9-10.3, L.9-10.5

A. How does Roosevelt craft his speech?

1. **Discuss:** In the first paragraph of his address, Roosevelt tries to grab his audience's attention by asserting his leadership. *Use Table A-1 to list some of the qualities of leadership he cites in the first paragraph of his address.* What assertions does he make about his own leadership qualities in that same paragraph?

2. **Discuss:** In the second paragraph of his address, Roosevelt uses figurative language, particularly metaphors (unusual comparisons) and hyperbole (exaggeration) as well as striking word choices to dramatize the gravity of the situation the nation is facing. *Use Table A-2 to discuss Roosevelt's use of language.*

3. **Write:** Consider Roosevelt's rhetorical choices for the opening paragraphs of his speech and write a short essay analyzing and evaluating their effect on his listeners (or readers today). *Use evidence from the Roosevelt address in your response.*

WHAT DO AMERICANS HAVE TO FEAR?

Table A-1: Roosevelt's Leadership

Leadership qualities	Assertions in the text about Roosevelt's leadership	What Roosevelt is trying to show the American people
decisive	"I will address them with a candor and a decision"	Roosevelt is trying to convince the American people that he is a leader who can make important decisions

Table A-2: Roosevelt's Figurative Language

Example of figurative language	Your understanding of what Roosevelt means	Your interpretation of why Roosevelt is using this sort of language here
"The means of exchange are frozen in the currents of trade."	Money or the market generally (the means of exchange) is not circulating as it should (it's frozen).	The image of winter freezing up the normal functions of business is powerfully negative and unnatural. Currents are not supposed to be frozen. Roosevelt is making clear that the situation is unnatural (and that he is going to fix the problem).

B. Afraid or not?

RL.9-10.1, RL.9-10.3, RL.9-10.4, RL.9-10.5, RL.9-10.9, RI.9-10.1, RI.9-10.2, RI.9-10.4, RI.9-10.9, W.9-10.1, W.9-10.4, W.9-10.5, W.9-10.9, SL.9-10.1, L.9-10.1, L.9-10.2, L.9-10.3, L.9-10.5, L.9-10.6

1. **Discuss:** In the first chapter of *To Kill a Mockingbird*, Scout informs the reader that "it was a time of vague optimism. . . . Maycomb County had recently been told that it had nothing to fear but fear itself." Based on the opening chapters of the novel, what sorts of struggles do the residents of Maycomb County seem to be facing? In your opinion, do they seem optimistic or afraid? *Use Table B-1 to collect and organize your responses.*

2. **Discuss:** Consider Roosevelt's inaugural address. He describes "the dark realities of the moment." What are those realities, as they are described in the inaugural address? What does the address itself tell you about the state of the nation in 1933? Based on what you can glean from the address, brainstorm a list of those realities.

    Realities facing the nation in 1933:
    1. unemployment
    2.
    3.
    4.
    5.

3. **Discuss:** In what ways is the nation's plight reflected in the world described in the opening chapters of *Mockingbird*? *Use Table B-2 to collect and organize your responses.*

4. **Write:** As the residents of Maycomb County confront the "dark realities" that Roosevelt describes in his inaugural address, do they seem optimistic or fearful? *Use evidence from Roosevelt and* Mockingbird *in your response.*

Table B-1: Optimistic or Not?

Character	Fears or struggles?	Evidence	Optimistic— yes or no?
Maycomb, the town	The town seems to be struggling economically and generally.	"Maycomb was an old town, but it was a tired old town."	no

Table B-2: "Dark Realities of the Moment"

Roosevelt's reality	Evidence from address	That reality reflected in Mockingbird	Evidence from Mockingbird
unemployment	"a host of unemployed citizens face the grim problem of existence"	People with jobs are suffering because the farmers were hit hard by the [stock market] crash. So it isn't that people are unemployed, but people are not doing well.	"Atticus said professional people were poor because the farmers were poor. As Maycomb County was farm country, nickels and dimes were hard to come by for doctors and dentists and lawyers."

C. Should we have faith in democracy?

> RL.9-10.1, RL.9-10.2, RL.9-10.9,
> RI.9-10.1, RI.9-10.2, RI.9-10.3, RI.9-10.5,
> RI.9-10.6, RI.9-10.9, W.9-10.1,
> W.9-10.4, W.9-10.5, W.9-10.7,
> W.9-10.8, W.9-10.9, SL.9-10.1, L.9-10.1,
> L.9-10.2, L.9-10.3, L.9-10.5, L.9-10.6

1. **Research and Discuss:** What is a democracy? What is a dictatorship? Use the Internet to conduct some basic research about the fundamental differences between a democracy and a dictatorship. *Use Table C-1 to collect and organize your research.*

2. **Research and Discuss:** What are some fundamental differences between the rules by which democracy functions in *Mockingbird* as compared with our democracy today? Hint: Use the Internet to research the rights and roles of black and white women and black men in the 1930s. *Use Table C-2 to collect and organize your research.*

3. **Discuss:** In *Mockingbird*, the children get a lesson on democracy from Miss Gates, who distinguishes between the U.S. democracy in which "we don't believe in persecuting anybody" and the German dictatorship of Hitler, which is, during the time of the novel, persecuting Jews. Why do you think Harper Lee includes this lecture from Miss Gates about Hitler at this point in the novel? Consider the irony of Miss Gates's lesson on American democracy. Who, within the novel, is treated unjustly by American democracy?

4. **Write:** In Roosevelt's inaugural address, he expresses his view of democracy: "We do not distrust the future of essential democracy." What do you think Harper Lee's point of view is on the issue of American democracy? Do you think Lee would agree with the faith Roosevelt expresses in democracy within his address? *Use evidence from Roosevelt,* Mockingbird, *and your research in your response.*

Table C-1: What Is a Democracy?

Democracy	Dictatorship
Leader is elected by the people	Leader takes power without any election (or without a fair and free election)

Table C-2: Democracy Now and Then

Democracy now	Democracy in the 1930s world of Mockingbird
All women and black men can serve on juries	Only white men could serve on juries

D. What is a good neighbor?

RL.9-10.1, RL.9-10.2, RL.9-10.3, RL.9-10.9,
RI.9-10.1, RI.9-10.2, RI.9-10.3, RI.9-10.5,
RI.9-10.6, RI.9-10.9, W.9-10.1, W.9-10.2,
W.9-10.4, W.9-10.5, W.9-10.9, SL.9-10.1,
L.9-10.1, L.9-10.2, L.9-10.3, L.9-10.5, L.9-10.6

In the middle of his inaugural address, Roosevelt references "the policy of the good neighbor": "the neighbor who resolutely respects himself and, because he does so, respects the rights of others—the neighbor who respects his obligations and respects the sanctity of his agreements in and with a world of neighbors."

1. **Discuss:** What is a good neighbor, according to Roosevelt? What are the characteristics of a good neighbor?

    A good neighbor . . .

    1. respects himself
    2.
    3.
    4.

2. **Discuss:** Who are good neighbors in *Mockingbird*? Who are bad neighbors in the world of the novel? *Use Table D-1 to collect and organize your responses.*

3. **Discuss:** In the last chapter of the novel, Scout discusses her relationship with Boo Radley:

    Neighbors bring food with death and flowers with sickness and little things in between. Boo was our neighbor. He gave us soap dolls, a broken watch and chain, a pair of good-luck pennies, and our lives. But neighbors give in return. We never put back into the tree what we took out of it: we had given him nothing, and it made me sad.

    Think about Scout's remarks here in relation to Roosevelt's ideas of the "good neighbor." How has Boo Radley been a "good neighbor"? Is Scout right when she says that she and Jem never gave Boo anything? Have they really been bad neighbors?

4. **Write:** Consider this policy in relation to the novel. Pick two characters and explore how one exemplifies Roosevelt's "good neighbor" while the other does not. *Use evidence from Roosevelt and* Mockingbird *in your response.*

Table D-1: Who Is a Good Neighbor?

Character	Good or bad neighbor?	Why?	Textual evidence
Jem	bad	Jem invades Boo Radley's privacy in the attempt to show Dill that he isn't afraid.	Jem threw open the gate and sped to the side of the house, slapped it with his palm and ran back past us.

E. What does it mean to be interdependent?

RL.9-10.1, RL.9-10.2, RL.9-10.3,
RL.9-10.9, RI.9-10.1, RI.9-10.2,
RI.9-10.3, RI.9-10.5, RI.9-10.6,
RI.9-10.9, W.9-10.1, W.9-10.2,
W.9-10.4, W.9-10.5, W.9-10.9,
SL.9-10.1, L.9-10.1, L.9-10.2,
L.9-10.3, L.9-10.5, L.9-10.6

Near the end of his inaugural address, Roosevelt speaks of "the interdependence of the various elements of all parts of the United States." Of this "interdependence," he says, "we now realize as we have never realized before our interdependence on each other; that we can merely take but we must give as well; that if we are to go forward, we must move as a trained and loyal army willing to sacrifice for the good of a common discipline."

1. **Discuss:** What does "interdependence" mean? What do you think Roosevelt means when he speaks of the interdependence of Americans? Do you think Roosevelt sees this interdependence as a strength or weakness? Why do you think Roosevelt suggests that the reality of American interdependence on each other is a new realization?

2. **Discuss:** In what ways are characters in *Mockingbird* interdependent? What are the consequences of their interdependence? *Use Table E-1 to collect and organize your responses.*

3. **Write:** Pick three examples in which characters embrace or reject their interdependence with others. How do these examples reflect on and perhaps complicate Roosevelt's idea that "interdependence" will allow us to "go forward" as a nation? *Use evidence from Roosevelt and* Mockingbird *in your response.*

Table E-1: What Does It Mean to Be Interdependent?

Character	Evidence or example	Interpretation	Consequences
Miss Maudie	The children are allowed to play in her yard: "we could play on her lawn, eat her scuppernongs if we didn't jump on the arbor, and explore her vast back lot." She also often bakes for them.	Miss Maudie lives alone and doesn't have children of her own. She seems to enjoy having the children be a part of her life. She embraces interdependence with Atticus's family.	Miss Maudie's embrace of interdependence seems to benefit both her and the children.

CLASS ACTIVITY

RL.9-10.1, RL.9-10.2, RL.9-10.3, RL.9-10.9, RI.9-10.1,
RI.9-10.2, RI.9-10.3, RI.9-10.4, RI.9-10.5, RI. 9-10.6, RI.9-10.8,
RI.9-10.9, W.9-10.1, W.9-10.2, W.9-10.3, W.9-10.4, W.9-10.5,
W.9-10.6, W.9-10.7, W.9-10.8, W.9-10.9, SL.9-10.1, SL.9-10.2,
SL.9-10.3, SL.9-10.4, SL.9-10.5, SL.9-10.6, L.9-10.1, L.9-10.2,
L.9-10.3, L.9-10.5, L.9-10.6

Task: Your goal is to produce a news report about FDR's first inaugural address. Your report must include:

1. **Footage of the Address.** You may pick and choose which sections of the address you want to include. You can videotape or record audio of someone in your group delivering the selections; alternatively, you may splice together online selections from Roosevelt's real speech.

2. **Interviews with five Maycomb residents.** You may pick which characters to feature, but your interviews should indicate how these residents respond to FDR's address. Be sure to ask them what they think of his address, how they feel the address responds to the needs and concerns of Maycomb, and how they feel about him as president. Conduct these interviews and then integrate them (audio, video, or text based) into your final news report.

3. **Other visuals.** Like any good news report, you want to include some pertinent and suggestive pictures that illustrate the issues in the story. Include visuals that reflect FDR's inauguration, the state of the country (the Depression), and life in places like Maycomb at the time.

4. **You will present your news report in class.** During your presentation, you will explain the components of your project, what choices you made, and what you were trying to accomplish. Be prepared to answer questions about your work.

In addition, each individual must produce:

5. **A narrative explanation.** Write a narrative in which you explain what your group was trying to accomplish and the choices you made in fulfilling the requirements of the assignment (your selections of the address; your pictures). Justify (with textual evidence) how the *Mockingbird* characters' responses to the interview questions make sense in terms of your larger understanding of them and the novel.

6. **A discussion of your group dynamic.** Write a narrative in which you explain your role in the group. What tasks did you take responsibility for? How successfully did you collaborate with your peers? What struggles did your group face in tackling the project?

CLASS ACTIVITY RUBRIC

Category	4—Excellent	3—Good	2—Satisfactory	1—Unsatisfactory
Address footage (strategic use of media in presentations; integration of diverse media)	Selections of FDR's address are well chosen and presented effectively	Selections of FDR's address are generally well chosen and presented effectively	Selections of FDR's address are somewhat well chosen and presented with limited effectiveness	Selections of FDR's address are not chosen or presented effectively
Interviews (determine the meaning of and analyze text)	Interviews show outstanding understanding of and insight into the texts and characters	Interviews show good understanding of and insight into the texts and characters	Interviews show limited or uneven understanding of and insight into the texts and characters	Interviews show insufficient or inaccurate understanding of and insight into the texts and characters
Visuals other than the address (strategic use of media in presentations; integration of diverse media)	Project makes effective use of strategic visuals and media other than the address	Project makes good use of strategic visuals and media other than the address	Project makes limited or uneven use of strategic visuals and media other than the address	Project makes insufficient or ineffective use of strategic visuals and media other than the address
Narrative explanation (cite relevant and sufficient textual evidence)	Narrative explanation is clear, coherent, and shows excellent insight into the texts	Narrative explanation is solid and shows good insight into the texts	Narrative limited or uneven explanation and shows some insight into the texts	Narrative explanation is unclear and/or incoherent and shows little insight into the texts
Collaboration (initiate and participate effectively in collaboration)	Student takes responsibility for his or her own work; collaborates well with others; negotiates group dynamics well	Student takes responsibility for his or her own work; collaborates sufficiently with others; shows some success negotiating group dynamics	Student takes limited responsibility for his or her own work; collaborates minimally with others; attempts to negotiate group dynamics	Student takes no responsibility for his or her own work; student does not collaborate with others; student struggles to or is unable to negotiate group dynamics
Vocabulary (use domain-specific vocabulary)	Several "words to own" from the unit are used correctly	Some "words to own" from the unit are used correctly in news report and/or narratives	One or more "words to own" from the unit are used but perhaps not correctly or effectively in news report and/or narratives	No "words to own" from the unit are used in news report and/or narratives
Class presentation (presentation of knowledge and ideas)	Presentation of the project is effective, concise, logical, and organized	Presentation of the project is generally but not fully effective, concise, logical, and organized	Presentation of the project is somewhat effective, but with some issues of brevity, logic, and organization	Presentation of the project is not effective, with serious problems in brevity, logic, and organization

UNIT 2

Who's Poor?

Jens Beckert, "Political Structure and Inheritance Law: The Abolition of Entails"

Overview

In chapter 2, Scout explains how she learned of the financial troubles the Cunningham family suffered due to the fact that their land was entailed. Though her understanding and explanation of it are incomplete, the concept of entailment is critical to our understanding of the Cunninghams' social position and to the larger social structure of the novel. When an estate was entailed, it could not be sold or broken up; it was passed down from one heir to the next, from generation to generation. Brought over from feudal Europe to colonial America, this legal instrument was used to keep land-based estates undivided. However, in practice, families sometimes ended up like the Cunninghams: rich in land, but poor in every other way because they could not sell off pieces of the estate to raise money to work on or develop the land. Entailments, widely considered antithetical to the ideals of democracy and equality, were generally abolished during the American Revolution, but remained in some form in Alabama and Mississippi.

Timing

These brief excerpts from Jens Beckert's book *Inherited Wealth* (2008) can be used as early as chapter 2 to help students understand entailment and its implications, but entailment is also mentioned in chapter 15 when Scout confronts the mob that has come to lynch Tom Robinson at the Maycomb jail.

Consider the following guidelines regarding when to undertake the different activities:

Essential question for discussion and writing	Objective	Suggested timing	Suggested rubric	Additional research
A. What is entailment and why is it so bad?	Students will (SW) analyze how entailment works as well as the criticism of entails in order to determine why they were abolished in America.	any time—this set of questions doesn't require any knowledge of *Mockingbird*	A	N
B. Why are the Cunninghams poor?	SW analyze the impact that entailment had on the Cunninghams' way of life in order to evaluate how it affected their status in the community.	after chapter 2 when Scout explains to Miss Caroline about the Cunninghams	B	Y
C. Why are the Ewells the "disgrace of Maycomb"?	SW analyze the differences between the Ewells and Cunninghams in order to determine why Atticus feels so differently about them.	after chapter 3 when Atticus describes the Ewells	A	N

Notes on the Article

- Entailment is a minor but interesting feature in Lee's novel, but one that students will almost certainly have no background knowledge about. It is worth examining what entailments were because, based on the limited discussion of them in the novel, students often misunderstand the complex social position of the Cunninghams in the world of the novel. There is also a fair amount of misinformation online about entailment and its meaning in *Mockingbird*, which we hope these materials will help you counter.

- The following excerpts from Beckert's book explain the effects of entailment and the reasons why people like economist and philosopher Adam Smith opposed them from the time the United States was founded.

- Because we think that the language in these excerpts is a bit tricky, we have included substantial scaffolding within the graphic organizers included in the writing and discussion activities. If you feel that your students can do this work more independently, the organizers could easily be tweaked for that purpose.
- These excerpts contain some legal terminology that students will need assistance in unpacking. Some of the key vocabulary offers opportunities to focus on secondary meanings of common words like "entail," "disposition," and "succeed" that students may not be familiar with and to develop understanding of multiple forms of certain words like "bequeath" and "bequest" and "function" and "dysfunctional."
- Key vocabulary: entail, testament, disposition, succeed, bequeath, subsequent, dynastic, repercussion, evident, conception, relic, feudal, function, capital, liberal, civic equality, meritocracy

Suggested Media Links
- *Downton Abbey*—season 1, episode 1: The tension of the series hinges upon the fact that Downton Abbey is entailed, which means that Lord Grantham's estate must pass to his nearest male heir, distant cousin Matthew Crawley. Because of the entail, Lord Grantham has no power over what happens to his estate and cannot bequeath it to his daughters.

VOCABULARY WARM-UP

Words to own: entail, testament, disposition, succeed, bequeath, subsequent, dynastic, repercussion, evident, conception, relic, feudal, function, capital, liberal, civic equality, meritocracy

Section A: Use context clues. Read the following sentences and use context clues to determine the meaning of the italicized words.

1. In his book *Inherited Wealth* Jens Beckert writes: "If real property is *entailed*, it cannot be sold by the owner of the *entail*; instead, it is passed on from generation to generation according to the succession determined by the founder." Based on the context in which it is used, what do you think an *entail* is? What does it mean if a property is *entailed*? Why would a founder want to *entail* his or her property? If you were someone who received property through an entail, what could you do with that property?

2. According to Beckert, "As a rule, the landed property was *bequeathed* to the eldest son and had to be passed on . . . to the next generation." Based on the context in which it is used, what do you think it means to *bequeath* something?

3. Beckert explains that "If real property is entailed . . . it is passed on from generation to generation according to the *succession* determined by the founder." Based on the context in which it is used, what do you think *succession* means?

4. According to Beckert, "Entails are a legal institution . . . through which the *testator* can control the use of his property across many generations, thereby exerting influence on the property relationships of the succeeding generations." Based on the context in which it is used, who is a *testator*? What would a *testator* use to express his or her wishes to succeeding generations?

5. As Beckert writes, "The preferential treatment of one social class in property law runs counter to the principle of *civic equality*." Based on the context in which it is used, what do you think *civic equality* is? Why would an entail run counter to *civic equality*?

Section B: More context clues. Here your task is to use context clues to understand the word's meaning and to practice your context clues skills.

1. After the courtroom was quiet again, the judge warned the spectators that she would clear the courtroom if any *subsequent* disruptions occurred. *Subsequent* here means
   a) violent
   b) rude
   c) further
   d) loud

2. Which word or phrase from the sentence in question 1 best helps the reader understand the meaning of *subsequent*?
   a) courtroom
   b) judge warned
   c) quiet again
   d) disruptions

3. The girl's happiness at being accepted by her first-choice college was *evident* from the huge smile on her face as she showed the letter to her parents. *Evident* here means
   a) equal
   b) exceptional
   c) caused by
   d) made clear by

4. Which word or phrase from the sentence in question 3 best helps the reader understand the meaning of *evident*?
   a) accepted
   b) huge smile on her face
   c) first-choice college
   d) showed the letter

Section C: Use the dictionary in order to understand the uncommon meanings of these common words.

1. Beckert writes that "family entails were the most important—and most controversial—instrument for placing testamentary restrictions on the heirs' rights of *disposition*." He is not referring to the heirs' attitudes. What does he mean by *disposition* in this case?

2. According to Beckert, "large-scale landholding led to an unproductive use of the land, because the owners had neither *capital* for, nor interest in, an efficient use." Beckert is not referring to the city where a state or federal government is located. What does *capital* refer to in this context?

3. "The growing criticism of entails expresses the spread of an individual *conception* of property," Beckert explains. He is not referring to *conception* in terms of pregnancy. What do you think Beckert means by an individual *conception* of property?

4. According to Beckert, "In the *liberal* worldview, the entail goes against civic equality, individual rights of freedom, . . . the process of economic modernization, and political democratization." The word *liberal* is often used to direct someone to apply a generous amount of something, like lotion, "apply *liberally*." However, this is not what Beckert is referring to. What does he mean by a *liberal* worldview? What kinds of things does a person with a *liberal* worldview believe?

Section D: Use the dictionary to look up the italicized words and answer the following questions based on their definitions.

1. If a dictator had *dynastic* ambitions, whom would he want to take power after his death? Why?

2. If you didn't fill out your college applications until the last minute, what might some of the *repercussions* be? Why?

3. If you told your friend that her outfit made her look like a *relic* from the 1960s, what would that mean? Do you think she would be happy or sad about your remark?

4. Would you want to live in a country with a *feudal* social and economic system? Why or why not?

5. Why might someone write a *testament*? What *function* would it serve?

6. Do you think it's good for a society to be a *meritocracy*? Do you think the United States is a *meritocracy*? Why or why not?

Section E: Practice using the word correctly by choosing the correct form of the word that best fits in the blank within the following sentences.

1. The Cunninghams could not sell their land because it had been _____ generations ago.
   a) entail
   b) entailment
   c) entailed
   d) entails

2. According to the _____ described in her uncle's will, she inherited all of his property.
   a) bequeath
   b) bequest
   c) bequeathed
   d) bequeathable

3. Though putting one person in charge was supposed to make decision-making easier, it actually caused a great deal of _____ in the group; nothing was accomplished.
   a) function
   b) functional
   c) dysfunction
   d) dysfunctional

4. Due to the entail placed on the property he had inherited from his father, he could not _____ of the estate as he saw fit; the property would automatically pass to his first-born son.
   a) disposition
   b) dispose
   c) disposal
   d) dispositions

Section F: Vocabulary skits. Use the model sentences and definitions to understand the words in question. Create a skit in which you address the given topic. Every member of the group must use the vocabulary word at least once during your performance of the skit.

1. *testament*—a will, particularly one that explains who should inherit one's property
   - The wealthy man's *testament* declared that he had willed all of his possessions to charity.
   - The family thought they knew what their father's *testamentary* intentions were, so they were shocked to find out that he had changed his will just before he died.
   - According to the lawyer, the *testator* had made sure that her will would withstand any legal challenges from her heirs.

   Scenario: Create a skit in which a group of family members listen to a lawyer read aloud their grandmother's last will and *testament*, which details who inherits what from her very large estate. Some are happy with what they have been bequeathed, while others feel unfairly slighted.

2. *repercussion*—the effect or consequence of an action or event
   - The boy realized that he had not sufficiently considered the possible *repercussions* of his actions when he saw the photos online of his foolish behavior at the party.
   - The senator thought about the devastating *repercussions* the law would have on the lives of people in his state and worked to make sure it was defeated.
   - Many scientists worry that the devastating *repercussions* of climate change may be irreversible unless we take action quickly.

   Scenario: Create a skit in which a group of teenagers is arguing about how one of their friends should respond after being insulted by one of their classmates. The friend is angry and wants to respond violently. Some of the teenagers agree, while others warn that the *repercussions* of doing so would bring even more grief.

3. *dysfunction*—something not working properly or the state of not working properly
   - While the girl agreed with her friend's point of view, she argued that responding with anger was *dysfunctional* and was only going to make the situation worse.
   - No matter how many times he had it fixed, the boy's computer seemed to be in a perpetual state of *dysfunction*.
   - The supervisor realized that her overly critical manner toward her employees was creating *dysfunction* in their office.

Scenario: Create a skit in which a group of teenagers is working on a project, but getting nowhere. They stop their work to talk and figure out what is making their group so *dysfunctional.*

4. *meritocracy*—a social system in which individuals are rewarded based on their talents and achievement, rather than family background or wealth

- The founders of the United States wanted the country to be a *meritocracy*, where opportunity and success was based more on achievement and less on birth and wealth as compared with England.
- Some argue that the rapidly increasing costs of college are making the United States less of a *meritocracy* because only students from more affluent backgrounds can afford a university education.
- Many immigrants come to the United States hoping to benefit from its *meritocratic* society; they believe that if they work hard, they will be rewarded.

Scenario: Create a skit in which a group of students has been marooned on a deserted island with little hope of rescue any time soon. They are debating what kind of society they should have. Some think that the students from wealthier backgrounds should be in charge and have the most privileges; others think the community should be a *meritocracy*, in which people are rewarded for their contributions.

ESSENTIAL QUESTION: WHO'S POOR?

Introduction

In this excerpt from his book *Inherited Wealth*, Professor Jens Beckert describes what it meant when property is entailed, as is the case with Walter Cunningham in *Mockingbird*. He explains that the practice of entailing land for one's heirs was brought over from Europe but came to be widely criticized during the colonial period by people as prominent as economist and philosopher Adam Smith. Entails were generally abolished right after the American Revolution, except in Alabama and Mississippi.

Political Structure and Inheritance Law: The Abolition of Entails

During the period under examination here, . . . family entails were the most important—and most controversial—instrument for placing testamentary restrictions on the heirs' rights of disposition. If real property is *entailed*, it cannot be sold by the owner of the entail; instead, it is passed on from generation to generation according to the *succession* determined by the founder. As a rule, the landed property was *bequeathed* to the eldest son and had to be passed on, in all *subsequent* successions to the next generation. Entails are a legal institution of *dynastic*

Reflect on the essential question: What does the question suggest to you?

Reflect on the introduction: The introduction tells you that entailments were abolished just after the American Revolution. If that was the case, why do you think Harper Lee mentions them in *Mockingbird*?

Reflect on the title: What does the title suggest about the relationship between political structure and inheritance law? What does the subtitle suggest about why entails might have been abolished?

Vocabulary: Beckert writes that entails "plac[ed] *testamentary* restrictions on the heirs' rights of *disposition*." What is a *testament*? What does it mean if an heir's rights of *disposition are restricted*? Put this into your own words.

Key idea: Beckert says that "if real property is *entailed*, it cannot be sold by the owner of the entail; instead, it is passed on from generation to generation according to the *succession* determined by the founder." Put this into your own words. What does it mean for a founder to determine the succession of his property? Why would he want to entail his property instead of simply bequeathing it to his heir?

Notice the figurative language Beckert uses here. Why does he describe the effect of entailment as a family's wealth being "directed by the '*dead hand*' of the person who established the entail"? What does he mean by this figure of speech?

---

bequest through which the *testator* can control the use of his property across many generations, thereby exerting influence on the property relationships of the *succeeding* generations. The wealth is directed by the "*dead hand*" of the person who established the entail.

[Beckert goes on to explain how entails were used in Europe during the eighteenth, nineteenth, and early twentieth centuries.]

Criticism of Entails

The growing criticism of entails expresses the spread of an individual *conception* of property, in which the restrictions on individual rights of *disposition* through entail constitute a violation of individual rights.

Second, criticism of entails is aimed at the special privileges for one class of property-owners embodied in this legal institution and at the political structures that are propped up by these privileges. The preferential treatment of one social class in property law runs counter to the principle of *civic equality*. . . .

This characteristic reference to the principle of legal equality and the economic *repercussions* of the entailment of property is especially *evident* in Adam Smith. In *The Wealth of Nations* . . . Smith described the entail as a *legal relic* of the *feudal* era. Its function lay in

Key idea: According to Beckert, the increasing criticism of entails had to do with "an individual *conception* of property." Why would an entail be at odds with an individual's rights of *disposition*? Whose right or interests had been considered more important than the individual's in the past?

Key idea: Beckert writes that criticism of entails was "aimed at the special privileges for one class of property-owners embodied in this legal institution and at the political structures that are propped up by these privileges." How would entailment, "this legal institution," create "special privileges" for land owners? Why would people in colonial America criticize this? What is *civic equality*? How would entails "run counter" to civic equality?

Notice the language Beckert uses to summarize Adam Smith's views on entails: "a *legal relic* of the *feudal* era." What does it mean to be a *legal relic*? What was the *feudal* era? Put Smith's opinion of entails in your own words.

Key idea: According to Smith, an entail's "function lay in securing the privileged status of the nobility, and it was simultaneously economically dysfunctional: large-scale landholding led to an unproductive use of the land, because the owners had neither *capital* for, nor interest in, an efficient use." Unpack this idea: (1) What was the purpose of entails? (2) What was dysfunctional about them and why?

Notice how Beckert uses Smith's ideas. Are these Smith's exact words? How can you tell? Beckert cites a 1978 edition of Smith's book originally published in 1776. What does "409–10" refer to?

securing the privileged status of the nobility, and it was simultaneously economically dysfunctional: large-scale landholding led to an unproductive use of the land, because the owners had neither *capital* for, nor interest in, an efficient use (Smith 1978 [1776], 409–10). . . .

In the *liberal* worldview, the entail goes against *civic equality*, individual rights of freedom, the concept of *meritocracy*, the process of economic modernization, and political democratization. Defenders of this legal institution noted that the nobility was an important pillar of the state, and that it could perform its political *functions* only on the basis of secure landed wealth.

> **Vocabulary:** According to Beckert, those who held a *liberal* worldview considered entails to be contradictory toward the "concept of *meritocracy*." How would the practice of entailing property go against *meritocracy*?
>
> **Key idea:** Beckert writes that "defenders of this legal institution noted that the nobility was an important pillar of the state, and that it could perform its political functions only on the basis of secure landed wealth." Put the arguments that supporters of entails used to defend them in your own words.

Beckert, Jens. *Inherited Wealth*. Princeton, NJ: Princeton UP, 2008: 114, 117–118. Print.

CHECK FOR UNDERSTANDING   RI.9-10.1, RI.9-10.4, RI.9-10.6

1. Beckert writes: "Entails are a legal institution of dynastic bequest through which the testator can control the use of his property across many generations, thereby exerting influence on the property relationships of the *succeeding* generations." By *succeeding* he likely means
   a) accomplished
   b) satisfied
   c) influential
   d) following

2. According to Beckert, "The growing criticism of entails expresses the spread of an individual *conception* of property." By *conception*, he likely means
   a) creation
   b) understanding
   c) contradiction
   d) ownership

3. According to Beckert, those with a "*liberal* worldview" criticized entails because they went "against civic equality, individual rights of freedom, the concept of meritocracy, the process of economic modernization, and political democratization." Which phrase best summarizes what someone with a "*liberal* worldview" is concerned about?
   a) acquisition of wealth
   b) gaining political power
   c) maintaining political and economic stability
   d) progress toward freedom and equality

4. Beckert's main goal in this excerpt from his book *Inherited Wealth* seems to be
   a) to persuade people to entail as much of their property as possible.
   b) to explain why entails were criticized and abolished in America.
   c) to explain why entails were so beneficial to the foundation of the United States.
   d) to argue for the abolishment of entails throughout America and Europe.

5. Beckert writes: "Defenders of this legal institution noted that the nobility was an important pillar of the state, and that it could perform its political functions only on the basis of secure landed wealth." In other words, supporters of entailment argued

   a) that the wealthy served an important political role in society and needed their land to be secure in order to do so.

   b) that the wealthy should be able to sell off or develop their land as they saw fit.

   c) that the legal institution was essential to the spread of democracy and equality.

   d) that the legal institution was essential to helping the wealthy maximize their political power and the value of their property.

WRITING AND DISCUSSION

RI.9-10.1, RI.9-10.2, RI.9-10.3, W.9-10.2 W.9-10.4, W.9-10.5, W.9-10.9, SL.9-10.1, L.9-10.1, L.9-10.2, L.9-10.3

A. What is so bad about entailment?

1. **Discuss:** In the beginning of this excerpt, Beckert defines what entailing an estate means for its heirs. *Use Table A-1 to clarify what it meant when property was entailed.*

2. **Discuss:** Beckert then describes the reasons that many people in colonial America criticized entails. *Use Table A-2 to explain each criticism and reflect on why people around the time of the American Revolution would have opposed entails for each reason.*

3. **Write:** How did entails work? What was so bad about them? Why would so many people have opposed them that they were almost entirely abolished immediately following the American Revolution? *Use evidence from the Beckert excerpt in your response.*

Table A-1: What Entailment Means

Textual evidence	In your own words
"If real property is *entailed*, it cannot be sold by the owner of the entail"	The person who inherits an entailed property cannot sell the property
An estate "is passed on from generation to generation according to the *succession* determined by the founder"	
"As a rule, the landed property was *bequeathed* to the eldest son and had to be passed on in all *subsequent* successions to the next generation."	
"The wealth is directed by the *'dead hand'* of the person who established the entail"	

Table A-2: What Did Colonial Americans Dislike about Entails?

Textual evidence	Explanation
"the restrictions on individual rights of *disposition* through entail constitute a violation of individual rights"	Individual freedom was considered one of the primary reasons the American colonies declared its independence from England. An entail might mean that your great-grandfather decided that your property would go to your first-born son on your death, even if you wanted to give it to your second-born son or daughter.
"criticism of entails is *aimed at the special privileges for one class of property-owners embodied in this legal institution and at the political structures that are propped up by these privileges*"	
"*it was simultaneously economically dysfunctional: large-scale landholding led to an unproductive use of the land, because the owners had neither capital for, nor interest in, an efficient use*"	
"In the *liberal* worldview, the entail goes against *civic equality*, individual rights of freedom, the concept of *meritocracy*, the process of economic modernization, and political democratization."	

B. Why are the Cunninghams poor?

RL.9-10.1, RL.9-10.2, RL.9-10.3, RL.9-10.4, RI.9-10.1, W.9-10.2, W.9-10.4, W.9-10.5, W.9-10.7, W.9-10.8, W.9-10.9, SL.9-10.1, L.9-10.1, L.9-10.2, L.9-10.3, L.9-10.4, L.9-10.5

1. **Discuss:** In chapter 2 of *Mockingbird*, Scout relates Jem's description of entailment as "a condition of having your tail in a crack." Based on what you know about entailment from the Beckert excerpt, is that figure of speech an accurate description? Why or why not?

2. **Discuss:** In this same scene, Scout explains how she had learned about the Cunninghams' entailment from Atticus. How has the entailment affected their way of life? How does this compare to what Beckert says about the effects of entails?

3. **Research:** Conduct some basic research into how and why the stock market crash and the Depression "hit farmers the hardest," as Atticus says.

4. **Write:** According to Atticus, "professional people were poor because the farmers were poor." How does this statement reflect Atticus's relationship with Walter Cunningham? In what other ways has the Cunninghams' entailment impacted their status in Maycomb society? *Use information about entailment from the Beckert excerpt and about the stock market crash and the Depression from your research as well as evidence from* Mockingbird *in your response.*

C. Why are the Ewells the "disgrace of Maycomb"?

RL.9-10.1, RL.9-10.2, RL.9-10.3, RL.9-10.4, W.9-10.1, W.9-10.2 W.9-10.4, W.9-10.5, W.9-10.9, SL.9-10.1, L.9-10.1, L.9-10.2, L.9-10.3, L.9-10.4, L.9-10.5

1. **Discuss:** On her first day of school, as described in chapters 2 and 3, Scout explains the attitudes and behavior of two students, Walter Cunningham and Burris Ewell, to their teacher, Miss Caroline. *Use Table C-1 to identify and interpret the differences between the two children.*

2. **Discuss:** In these same two chapters, Atticus describes the Cunningham and the Ewell families. *Use Table C-2 to identify the characteristics Atticus attributes to each family.* What do you think about Atticus's different attitudes toward the two families? Why do you think his attitudes are so different?

3. **Write:** Why are the Ewells the "disgrace of Maycomb"? What makes the poverty of the Ewells different from the poverty of the Cunninghams? What place do you think the Cunninghams' entailment has in how they are treated and viewed by Atticus and others in the community? *Use evidence from* Mockingbird *and the Beckert excerpt in your response.*

Table C-1: Walter Cunningham versus Burris Ewell

Walter Cunningham		Burris Ewell	
Textual evidence	*Interpretation*	*Textual evidence*	*Interpretation*
"If Walter had owned any shoes he would have worn them the first day of school and then discarded them until mid-winter. He did have on a clean shirt and neatly mended overalls."	Walter and his family are very poor, but they are proud enough to make sure he is as presentable as possible on the first day of school.	"The cootie's host [Burris Ewell] showed not the faintest interest in the furor he had wrought. He searched the scalp above his forehead, located his guest and pinched it between his thumb and forefinger."	Burris has lice and doesn't care what anyone thinks of him or how ill-groomed he might be.
Walter doesn't have lunch and refuses the quarter Miss Caroline offers: "Nome thank you ma'am."		"He was the filthiest human I had ever seen. His neck was dark gray, the backs of his hands were rusty, and his fingernails were black deep into the quick. He peered at Miss Caroline from a fist-sized clean space on his face."	

Table C-1: Walter Cunningham versus Burris Ewell (continued)

Walter Cunningham		Burris Ewell	
Textual evidence	Interpretation	Textual evidence	Interpretation

Table C-2: Atticus's View of the Cunninghams and Ewells

The Cunninghams		The Ewells	
Textual evidence	*Interpretation*	*Textual evidence*	*Interpretation*
Atticus tells Mr. Cunningham to let paying him "be the least of your worries" and assures Scout that Mr. Cunningham will pay him, "not in money . . . but before the year's out I'll have been paid. You watch."	Atticus understands and is sympathetic to the Cunninghams' situation, and knows that Mr. Cunningham will make good on his debt.	"Atticus said the Ewells were the disgrace of Maycomb for three generations. None of them had done an honest day's work in his recollection."	Atticus condemns the way that the Ewells have never tried to improve themselves or undertaken any respectable kind of labor.
"The Cunninghams are country folks, farmers, and the crash hit them hardest."		"He said that some Christmas, he would take me with him and show me where and how they lived. They were people, but they lived like animals."	

Does a Girl Have to Be a Lady?

Lillian Eichler, Book of Etiquette

TEACHER'S GUIDE
Overview

During the course of *To Kill a Mockingbird*, Scout confronts, and often flouts, expectations for her behavior as a Southern girl from a respectable family. Many of these expectations are reflected in the following excerpt from Lillian Eichler's 1921 *Book of Etiquette*, which sold more than two million copies. Discussion of these ideals will enhance students' understanding of the context in which Scout is growing up in terms of gender roles and expectations. Students may also find the story behind Eichler's bestselling guide interesting (see introduction to excerpt). Eichler was only nineteen when the first volume was published.

Timing

This excerpt from Eichler's book on etiquette can be used as early as chapter 9 when Scout goes to Finch's Landing for Christmas Day, but students will have more to compare with Eichler's advice after reading chapter 13, when Aunt Alexandra comes to live with Scout and her family, or after chapter 24, when Scout participates in Aunt Alexandra's missionary circle meeting.

Consider the following guidelines regarding when to undertake the different activities:

Essential question for discussion and writing	Objective	Suggested timing	Suggested rubric	Additional research
A. What does it mean for a child to "be natural"?	Students will (SW) analyze Eichler's language in order to identify what is considered "natural" for children, especially girls.	any time—this set of questions doesn't require any knowledge of *Mockingbird*	A	N
B. How should a parent raise a child?	SW analyze Eichler's advice in order to use it in evaluating the parenting practices and philosophies of Atticus and Aunt Alexandra in relation to Scout.	after chapter 9 when Scout spends Christmas at Finch's Landing, or chapter 13, when Aunt Alexandra comes to stay with Scout and Jem	A	N
C. What are good manners for girls?	SW use their understanding of Eichler's advice in order to evaluate the behavior of the women at Aunt Alexandra's missionary circle meeting.	after chapter 24, when Scout attends the missionary circle meeting	A	N
D. Was life the same for girls as it was for boys?	SW research women's career opportunities in the 1930s in order to determine whether Scout would have had the same opportunities as Jem, as Eichler suggests.	after chapter 24, when Miss Stephanie asks Scout if she's going to be a lawyer	B	Y
Class Activity				
Letters to/from Lillian Eichler	SW use their understanding of Eichler's advice and the novel in order to draft letters from Aunt Alexandra, Scout, and/or Mayella Ewell to Eichler and responses from Eichler to each of them.	after chapter 24, when Scout attends the missionary circle meeting	rubric included	N

Notes on the Article

- Reading this piece will help students think about and understand how much gender roles and expectations have changed since the 1930s, particularly for girls and women. This excerpt from chapter 7 on "Parents and Children" includes the sections in which Eichler voices her specific mandates on how girls should be encouraged to behave.

- These sections of Eichler's text should provoke interesting discussion because, while her final pronouncements in this excerpt are clearly aligned with Aunt Alexandra's point of view that girls should wear dresses and behave like a lady, some of Eichler's earlier language could be used by Scout to argue that she should be allowed to be herself.

- Key vocabulary: etiquette, stilted, well-bred, repressed, implicit, husk, distinction, idle, proportion, repose, conception, ostentatious

Suggested Media Links

- An instructional video on YouTube on dating for 1940s and 1950s teens focuses on the boy's point of view but depicts quite a bit about how girls should appear and behave.

- The Emily Post Productions channel on YouTube features videos on how the French word "etiquette" came to be associated with manners, as well as tips for appropriate behavior in common present-day situations.

- Emily Post narrates a 1947 video on table manners on the Internet Archive (archive .org).

- A 1940 short film called "Easy Does It" on archive.org measures the effort required in women's domestic work and how modern devices are easing that burden. While not focused specifically on etiquette, the film reveals a great deal about gender roles at the time.

- The National Women's History Museum has a virtual exhibit on "A History of Women in Industry" on its website, featuring a section on the Depression era that offers useful information about the opportunities women in the 1930s had for working outside the home.

VOCABULARY WARM-UP

L.9-10.4, L.9-10.5, L.9-10.6

> **Words to own**: etiquette, stilted, well-bred, repressed, implicit, husk, distinction, idle, proportion, repose, conception, ostentatious

Section A: Use context clues. Read the following sentences and use context clues to determine the meaning of the italicized words.

1. In the preface to her 1921 *Book of Etiquette*, Lillian Eichler writes that "There are certain little courteous observances, certain social formalities that bespeak the true lady, the true gentleman. Some of us call it good form. Some of us call it culture. Some of us call it *etiquette*. But we all admit that it makes the world a better place to live in." Based on the context in which it is used, what do you think *etiquette* means? Do you agree with Eichler that *etiquette* makes "the world a better place to live in"? Why or why not?

2. According to Eichler, "*Stilted*, party-mannered children are bores. They are unnatural." Based on the context in which it is used, what do you think *stilted* means? Is Eichler saying that children who act in a *stilted* way are likeable or not? Why?

3. Eichler warns that shy children end up that way because "they are *repressed* instead of developed. Their natural tendencies are held down by constant reminders and scoldings and warnings." Based on the context in which it is used, what does it mean to be *repressed*? Why might being *repressed* make a child become shy?

4. Eichler distinguishes between two types of girls: "those who face life as some great opportunity, who consider it a splendid gift to be made the most of, and who help to create the beauty that they love to admire; and those who are butterflies of society, whose lives are mere *husks*, without depth, without worth-while impulses and ambitions." What does Eichler mean by the word *husks* here? What type of girl does Eichler prefer? Why?

Section B: More context clues. Here your task is to use context clues to understand the word's meaning and to practice your context clues skills.

1. There was an *implicit* loyalty among the group of friends; even without saying anything, they all just knew they would stick together. *Implicit* here means
   a) shaky
   b) unspoken
   c) untested
   d) equal

2. Which word or phrase from the sentence in question 1 best helps the reader understand the meaning of *implicit*?
   a) group of friends
   b) stick together
   c) just knew
   d) loyalty

3. Good manners are a mark of *distinction*; people who are always polite in social situations stand out from the crowd. *Distinction* here means
   a) distraction
   b) disorder
   c) difference
   d) perseverance

4. Which word or phrase from the sentence in question 3 best helps the reader understand the meaning of *distinction*?
   a) crowd
   b) polite
   c) social
   d) stand out

Section C: Use the dictionary in order to understand the uncommon meanings of these common words.

1. Eichler describes the conversation of certain girls as "*idle* chatter" and says that "their ambitions are to be 'social queens,' to earn social distinction and importance." She does not mean that the girls' chatter is inactive or unemployed. What does she mean by *idle* in this case?

---

2. Eichler would advise a young girl to "look to the ancient Greeks for inspiration. Here she will find the true *conception* of beauty." Eichler is not using *conception* in terms of pregnancy. What does *conception* refer to in this context?

Section D: Use the dictionary to look up the italicized words and answer the following questions based on their definitions.

1. Would you say that you dress in an *ostentatious* way? Why or why not?

2. What characteristics would you expect of someone who is *well-bred*? Why?

3. If your spending habits are out of *proportion* with your budget, what would that mean? Would it be good or bad? Why?

4. If you had a friend who was acting in a *stilted* way, what would you say to him? Why might he be acting this way?

5. In whom or what do you have *implicit* faith? Why?

6. What kinds of topics would you expect someone engaging in *idle* chatter to discuss? Why?

Section E: Practice using the word correctly by choosing the correct form of the word that best fits in the blank within the following sentences.

1. Even when the twins are standing next to each other, it's difficult to _____ between them.
   a) distinguish
   b) distinction
   c) distinctly
   d) distinguished

2. My best friend and I trust each other _____; even without talking about it, we know we can rely on each other for anything.
   a) implicit
   b) implicitness
   c) implicitly
   d) implicity

3. Many people have immigrated to the United States throughout its history in order to escape political _____ in their own countries.
   a) repress
   b) represses
   c) repressed
   d) repression

4. According to the rules of the U.S. judicial system, the sentence must be _____ to the severity of the crime.
   a) proportion
   b) proportionate
   c) proportionless
   d) proportions

Section F: Vocabulary skits. Use the model sentences and definitions to understand the words in question. Create a skit in which you address the given topic. Every member of the group must use the vocabulary word at least once during your performance of the skit.

1. *stilted*—stiffly dignified, overly formal, unnatural
   - His manner was so *stilted* at the beginning of the job interview, his prospective employer urged him to relax and act more like himself.
   - The politician's *stilted* language alienated the people she was trying to persuade to support her campaign; they felt like she was wooden and artificial.
   - The girl was so worried about acting appropriately during her first dinner with her boyfriend's parents that she seemed a bit *stilted* and overly polite.

   Scenario: Create a skit in which some teenagers are trying to help a friend figure out the best way to ask out someone he likes. Some of them think he should quote some poetry and use big words; others warn him that he might come off as too *stilted*.

2. *ostentatious*—eye-catching or striking dress or behavior intended to attract notice, showy
   - The bride did not appreciate her sister's *ostentatious* dress and behavior; she felt like her sister was trying to upstage her at her own wedding.
   - For some people, acting *ostentatiously* and wearing flamboyant styles comes naturally; these people may attract attention, but they are just expressing who they are.
   - While many Muslim women cover themselves in traditional black scarves and robes, they sometimes wear unexpectedly *ostentatious* clothing underneath.

Scenario: Create a skit in which a group of teenagers is arguing about what kinds of styles to wear to prom. Some of them want to wear something *ostentatious* that people will notice and remember, while others think it's better to wear something more classic and understated.

3. *repose*—a dignified, calm or peaceful manner or state
   - His meditative *repose* was broken by a crash of dishes from the kitchen.
   - Though the reporter kept asking the celebrity very sensitive questions, she maintained her *repose* throughout the interview and refused to let him upset her.
   - I enjoy walking in the woods because it allows me to clear my thoughts and achieve a peaceful *repose*.

Scenario: Create a skit in which a teenager is trying to meditate before a big test, while her friends are determined to disrupt her *repose* by making her laugh.

4. *idle*—of no real value or importance
   - The actress dismissed the rumors about her marriage breaking up as *idle* gossip.
   - The lawyer asked the judge to strike the witness's comments from the record because they were *idle* speculation and not based on known fact.
   - Because she kept going on and on about such *idle* matters, she was very boring to listen to.

Scenario: Create a skit in which one or more students criticize a small group of students for always talking about fashion and celebrity gossip. They argue that they shouldn't waste their time on such *idle* nonsense, while the others argue that such topics are important.

ESSENTIAL QUESTION: DOES A GIRL HAVE TO BE A LADY?
Introduction

In this excerpt from her first volume on social conduct, Lillian Eichler offers her opinions on how children, particularly girls, should behave. Eichler was an eighteen-year-old advertising copywriter when she was asked to write an updated guide on *etiquette* to replace one that had been written pre-1900 and was considered old-fashioned. Her *Book of Etiquette* was published in 1921 and sold more than two million copies in two years, making her a millionaire at the age of nineteen.

> **Reflect on the essential question:** What does the question suggest to you? What are the differences between a girl and a lady or between a woman and a lady? *Journal/gps*
>
> **Reflect on the introduction:** The introduction tells you that Eichler's book on social conduct was a bestseller. Why do you think it was so successful?

Chapter VII
Parents and Children
Let the Child Be Natural

After all, the greatest charm of childhood is natural, spontaneous simplicity. *Stilted*, party-mannered children are bores. They are unnatural. And that which is not natural, cannot be *well-bred*.

The cause of shy, bashful, self-conscious youngsters is wrong training. They are *repressed* instead of developed. Their natural tendencies are held down by constant reminders and scoldings and warnings. Instead, they should be *brought out* by proper encouragement, by kind, sympathetic understanding. Some children have the idea, in their extreme youth, that parents are made only to forbid things, to repress them and make them do things against which their natures revolt. The bond that should exist between parent and child is a certain understanding friendliness—an *implicit* faith on the part of the child, and a wise guidance on the part of the parent.

Remember that a child is like a flower. If the flower is not permitted to struggle upward towards the sun, and to gather in the tiny dewdrops, it will wither and die. If the child is not allowed to develop naturally, its tastes and ideals will be warped and shallow.

> **Reflect on the subtitle:** Eichler urges parents to "let the child be natural." What do you think she means by this? Why would she advise parents to do this?
>
> **Vocabulary:** Eichler says that, "Stilted, party-mannered children are bores. They are unnatural. And that which is not natural, cannot be well-bred." Put this into your own words.
>
> **Key idea:** Eichler says that children are sometimes shy because they have been *repressed* by too much scolding by adults. She argues that "they should be *brought out* by proper encouragement, by kind, sympathetic understanding." What does she mean by *"brought out"*? Does this advice seem surprising in a book of etiquette? Why or why not?

May be photocopied for classroom use. *Using Informational Text to Teach* To Kill a Mockingbird by Audrey Fisch and Susan Chenelle © 2014 (Lanham, MD: Rowman & Littlefield).

Teach your child to be well-mannered and polite, but do not disguise him with unnatural manners and speech.

The Young Girl

There are two kinds of young girls—those who face life as some great opportunity, who consider it a splendid gift to be made the most of, and who help to create the beauty that they love to admire; and those who are butterflies of society, whose lives are mere *husks*, without depth, without worth-while impulses and ambitions. They are satisfied if they know how to dance gracefully, if they know how to enter a room in an impressive manner, if they know how to be charming at the dinner table. Their conversation is *idle* chatter; their ambitions are to be "social queens," to earn social *distinction* and importance.

Fortunately, the twentieth century girl is less of a butterfly than the tight-laced hoop-skirted young miss of the latter part of the nineteenth century. Perhaps the war had something to do with it. Perhaps it is because so many new occupations have been opened up to her. Perhaps it is evolution. But the young miss of to-day is certainly more thrilled with life and its possibilities than her sister of two or three decades ago ever was.

Life is no longer shown to the young daughter as a plaything by fond parents who plan no future except marriage and social success for the young woman whose future rests in their hands. To-day life is shown to her as it is shown to her brother—as something beautiful, something impressive, something worthy of deep thought and ambitious plan.

To-day the young girl is not only taught to dance gracefully, to enter a room correctly, and to conduct herself with ease and charm at the dinner table, but she is taught

Vocabulary: Eichler says that the relationship between parents and children should be based on "*implicit* faith on the part of the child, and a wise guidance on the part of the parent." Put this into your own words.

Notice the simile here: "Remember *that a child is like a flower.*" What does Eichler mean by this figure of speech?

Key idea: Eichler makes a distinction between two types of young girls. Describe these two types in your own words. Which of these does Eichler prefer? Why?

Notice the metaphors Eichler uses in describing the girls she calls "butterflies of society." She goes on to say that their "lives are mere *husks.*" What does she mean by these figures of speech?

Key idea: Eichler goes on to describe the ideal twentieth-century girl and the opportunities she has. What reasons does she offer for why girls have changed since the end of the nineteenth century? Why do you think these would have impacted young girls in these ways?

to develop her natural talents and abilities so that the world will be left a little better for her having lived in it. Her conduct, therefore, is tinged with a new dignity of purpose, a new desire to make the best of the gift of life. Instead of *idle* chatter her conversation assumes the *proportion* of intellectual discussion, and young men and women to-day discuss intelligently problems that would not have been mentioned in polite society a generation ago.

It is to help the young girl to prepare for the glorious future that awaits her that the following paragraphs are written.

The Girl's Manners

There is nothing quite as charming in a young girl as *repose* of manner. A soft voice, a quiet, cultured manner is more to be admired than a pretty face, or an elaborate gown.

Let the young girl look to the ancient Greeks for inspiration. Here she will find the true *conception* of beauty—*repose* of manner and utter simplicity. She will find that to be perfect is to be natural, and that one must be simple and *unostentatious* to be beautiful in the true sense of the word. After all, what can be quite so lovely as beautiful manners? And what can be more worthy of admiration and respect than a sweet, well-mannered young girl?

Politeness and courtesy are two other important virtues that the young girl should develop. She should be as polite to her mother and sister as she is to strangers. She should be courteous and kind to everyone. And she should learn the art of listening as well as the art of conversation.

Reflect: Eichler argues that "To-day life is shown to [a girl] as it is shown to her brother." Does this mean that girls and boys, or men and women, were equal in the early twentieth century?

Reflect: Why do you think Eichler segues into the next section with this last sentence about helping young girls? What is she preparing her reader for?

Notice that Eichler encourages young girls to "look to the ancient Greeks for inspiration." Why do you think she would urge them to emulate the ancient Greeks?

Vocabulary: Eichler says that young girls "will find the true conception of beauty" in the "repose of manner and utter simplicity" of the ancient Greeks, and that "she will find that to be perfect is to be natural, and that one must be simple and *unostentatious* to be natural." Put this into your own words.

Key point: In addition to a simple, natural manner, Eichler advises young girls to cultivate politeness, courtesy, kindness and good listening and conversational skills. How do you think Scout would feel about this section of Eichler's guide? Why?

Eichler, Lillian. *Book of Etiquette.* Vol. 1. New York: Nelson Doubleday, 1921. 271–274. Print.

CHECK FOR UNDERSTANDING   RI.9-10.1, RI.9-10.4, RI.9-10.6

1. Eichler writes: "The bond that should exist between parent and child is a certain understanding friendliness—an *implicit* faith on the part of the child, and a wise guidance on the part of the parent." By *implicit*, she likely means
   a) unbreakable
   b) important
   c) understood
   d) submissive

2. Eichler writes: "She will find that to be perfect is to be natural, and that one must be simple and unostentatious to be beautiful in the true sense of the word." By *unostentatious*, she means
   a) perfect
   b) beautiful
   c) truthful
   d) plain

3. According to Eichler, there are some girls "who are *butterflies of society*, whose lives are mere *husks*, without depth, without worth-while impulses and ambitions." Which word best describes this type of girl?
   a) superficial
   b) ambitious
   c) intellectual
   d) sensitive

4. Eichler's main goal in this excerpt from her *Book of Etiquette* seems to be
   a) to speak out about the poor behavior of twentieth-century girls.
   b) to urge parents to let girls be themselves and do whatever they want.
   c) to urge parents to help their daughters cultivate lives of purpose and dignity.
   d) to urge parents to shelter their daughters from the evil influences of the outside world.

5. Eichler writes: "To-day life is shown to her as it is shown to her brother—as something beautiful, something impressive, something worthy of deep thought and ambitious plan." By this statement, she is trying to assert
   a) that girls and boys have different roles in today's society.
   b) that girls should support the ambitions of the men in their lives.
   c) that girls should focus on making things beautiful in the world.
   d) that girls can now engage meaningfully with the world, just as their brothers do.

WRITING AND DISCUSSION

RI.9-10.1, RI.9-10.2, RI.9-10.3, RI.9-10.4, RI.9-10.5, RI.9-10.6, W.9-10.2 W.9-10.4, W.9-10.5, W.9-10.9, SL.9-10.1, L.9-10.1, L.9-10.2, L.9-10.3, L.9-10.4, L.9-10.5

A. What does it mean for a child to "be natural"?

1. **Discuss:** Eichler begins this chapter of her book by advising parents to "Let the child be natural." *Use Table A-1 to identify the qualities and behaviors Eichler considers in the "Let the Child Be Natural" section to be natural and unnatural.* Why do you think Eichler uses the word "natural"?

2. **Discuss:** In paragraph 3, Eichler compares a child to a flower. How does she use this particular metaphor to advance her argument? In paragraph 5, Eichler discusses girls who are the "butterflies of society" and whose lives are "mere husks." How does this second metaphor function in her argument? Compare Eichler's use of these two different metaphors in her discussion.

3. **Write:** Throughout this excerpt, Eichler builds upon her advice to parents to let their children "be natural." Consider Eichler's rhetorical choices as she articulates this idea. How does she use metaphorical language to define some qualities and behaviors as "natural" for young women? *Use evidence from the excerpt in your response.*

Table A-1: What Does It Mean to Be Natural?

Natural	Unnatural
"spontaneous simplicity"	"stilted, party-mannered"

B. How should a parent raise a child?

RL.9-10.1, RL.9-10.2, RL.9-10.3, RI.9-10.1,
RI.9-10.2, RI.9-10.3, RI.9-10.5, RI.9-10.6,
W.9-10.1, W.9-10.4, W.9-10.5, W.9-10.9,
SL.9-10.1, L.9-10.1, L.9-10.2

1. **Discuss:** Eichler begins this chapter of her book with advice for parents. *Use Table B-1 to list the qualities of well-bred and ill-bred children and their relationships with their parents.* How would you summarize Eichler's overall advice for parents on raising their children?

2. **Discuss:** Atticus and Aunt Alexandra often clash on how to raise children, particularly Scout, throughout *Mockingbird.* How do you think their parenting styles accord with Eichler's advice and recommendations? *Use Table B-2 to compare the parenting philosophies of Eichler, Atticus, and Aunt Alexandra.*

3. **Write:** Consider Eichler's advice for parents. What would she have thought of Atticus's and Aunt Alexandra's parenting philosophies and practices? *Use evidence from* Mockingbird *and Eichler's excerpt in your response.*

Table B-1: How Does Good Parenting Produce Good Children?

Types of children and their qualities	Treatment from parents	Relationship with parents
Well-bred: natural, spontaneous charm, but well-mannered and polite	"*brought out* by proper encouragement, by kind, sympathetic understanding"	"a certain understanding friendliness—an implicit faith on the part of the child, and a wise guidance on the part of the parent"
Ill-bred:		

Table B-2: How Should Children Be Raised?

Eichler's advice	Atticus's opinion	Specific evidence or example	Aunt Alexandra's opinion	Specific evidence or example
"[Children] should be *brought out* by proper encouragement, by kind, sympathetic understanding" not "constant reminders and scoldings and warnings."	Atticus listens to his children and guides them in developing their own moral judgments	Atticus teaches Scout: "You never really understand a person until you consider things from his point of view"	Aunt Alexandra believes in manners and moral absolutes	Aunt Alexandra "had river-boat, boarding school manners; let any moral come along and she would uphold it"
"The bond that should exist between parent and child is a certain understanding friendliness—an *implicit* faith on the part of the child, and a wise guidance on the part of the parent."				

C. What are good manners for girls?

RL.9-10.1, RL.9-10.2, RL.9-10.3, RI.9-10.1, RI.9-10.2, RI.9-10.3, RI.9-10.6, W.9-10.1, W.9-10.4, W.9-10.5, W.9-10.9, SL.9-10.1, L.9-10.1, L.9-10.2

1. **Discuss:** Before addressing the topic of "The Girl's Manners," Eichler explains her purpose: "It is to help the young girl to prepare for the glorious future that awaits her that the following paragraphs are written." List the particular manners or qualities that Eichler insists are important for the young girl. Why do you think Eichler insists on these very traditionally feminine manners for girls even while insisting that life today is different and full of opportunity for the girl, "shown to her as it is shown to her brother"?

   Important qualities or manners for the young girl:
   a. a soft voice
   b.
   c.
   d.

2. **Discuss:** In chapter 24, Scout joins Aunt Alexandra's missionary circle, where she does her best to fulfill her aunt's expectations in terms of her manners and appearance and also gets to observe the manners of other women. *Use Table C-1 to identify and interpret the good or bad manners exhibited in this chapter.*

3. **Discuss:** At the end of chapter 24, Aunt Alexandra is shaken and distraught over the news of Tom Robinson's death. Yet Aunt Alexandra and Scout try to practice good manners in this moment. Scout says, "if Aunty could be a lady at a time like this, so could I." Why do you think Aunt Alexandra strives to practice good manners at this moment? Why do you think Scout tries to emulate her? What do you think of their behavior in this moment?

4. **Write:** Use Eichler to consider the manners of Scout, Aunt Alexandra, and the women at Aunt Alexandra's missionary circle. Who would Eichler think best illustrates "good manners"? What do you think Scout learns about manners in this chapter? What do you think about the role of manners in this chapter? *Use evidence from* Mockingbird *and Eichler's excerpt in your response.*

Table C-1: Good or Bad Manners?

Character	Action	Textual evidence	Good or bad manners?	Interpretation
Scout	Scout wears her Sunday dress, shoes, and petticoat, but with her britches underneath.	"You're mighty dressed up, Miss Jean Louise," she said. "Where are your britches today?" "Under my dress."	Good	Scout is trying to please Aunt Alexandra and fit in, but she can't help being herself.
Miss Maudie	Miss Maudie supports Scout when Miss Stephanie is interrogating her about growing up to be a lawyer.			
Miss Stephanie				
Aunt Alexandra				
Mrs. Merriweather				
Calpurnia				

D. Was life the same for girls as it was for boys?

RL.9-10.1, RL.9-10.2, RL.9-10.3, RI.9-10.1, RI.9-10.2, RI.9-10.3, W.9-10.1, W.9-10.4, W.9-10.5, W.9-10.7, W.9-10.8, W.9-10.9, SL.9-10.1, L.9-10.1, L.9-10.2

1. **Discuss:** Eichler argues that, as of the time she was writing, the early 1920s, "To-day life is shown to [a girl] as it is shown to her brother—as something beautiful, something impressive, something worthy of deep thought and ambitious plan." She also says: "Life is no longer shown to the young daughter as a plaything by fond parents who plan no future except marriage and social success for the young woman whose future rests in their hands." Unpack these lines. What do they tell you about expectations for girls before the 1920s? Do you think Eichler is suggesting that as of "To-day," the 1920s, girls and boys have equal opportunities?

2. **Discuss:** While visiting Finch's Landing for Christmas in chapter 9, Scout encounters various social expectations based on gender. *Use Table D-1 to identify and analyze these expectations.*

3. **Research:** Research the kinds of career opportunities women had in the 1930s. What developments occurred in the United States in the 1920s and 1930s that helped to shape these opportunities for American women around the time Eichler was writing?

4. **Write:** Using what you have learned from Eichler and your research, discuss the expectations and opportunities for Scout. Is life the same for Scout as it is for Jem? Can Scout expect the same opportunities and future as her brother? *Use evidence from* Mockingbird, *Eichler's excerpt, and your research in your response.*

Table D-1: Are Boys and Girls Treated Equally?

Event	Textual evidence	Equal or unequal?	Interpretation
Uncle Jack tries to convince Scout to stop cursing so that she can be a young lady	"Scout, you'll get into trouble if you go around saying things like that. You want to grow up to be a lady, don't you?"	Unequal	Uncle Jack acts upon his view that cursing is less acceptable for girls than boys
Both Scout and Jem get air rifles for Christmas from Atticus	"they were from Atticus . . . and they were what we had asked for."	Equal	Atticus doesn't differentiate between his children in terms of gender in this regard

CLASS ACTIVITY

RL.9-10.1, RL.9-10.2, RL.9-10.3, RI.9-10.1, RI.9-10.2, RI.9-10.3, RI.9-10.5, RI. 9-10.6, RI.9-10.8, W.9-10.1, W.9-10.4, W.9-10.5, W.9-10.6, W.9-10.9, SL.9-10.1, SL.9-10.4, SL.9-10.6, L.9-10.1, L.9-10.2, L.9-10.6

Option 1: Imagine that Aunt Alexandra and Scout have each written to Eichler asking for help in their ongoing arguments about Scout's manners and behavior, citing the parts of Eichler's guide that they each agree with. Your task is to write these two letters and then draft a response from Eichler to each of them. Would you help them find common ground, or would you side with one or the other?

Option 2: Imagine that you are Mayella Ewell. What would you think of Eichler's advice? How relevant would it be to your life? Write a letter from Mayella to Eichler and then draft a response from Eichler back to Mayella.

Presentation: You will present your letters to the class, explain their components and the choices you made, and what arguments you were trying to make and how. Be prepared to answer questions about your work.

In addition, each individual must produce:

1. **A narrative explanation.** Write a narrative in which you explain what your group was trying to accomplish and the choices you made in fulfilling the requirements of the assignment. Justify (with textual evidence) how your responses make sense in terms of your understanding of both Eichler's advice and the debate over behavior and manners that occurs throughout the novel.

2. **A discussion of your group dynamic.** Write a narrative in which you explain your role in the group. What tasks did you take responsibility for? How successfully did you collaborate with your peers? What struggles did your group face in tackling the project?

CLASS ACTIVITY RUBRIC

Category	4—Excellent	3—Good	2—Satisfactory	1—Unsatisfactory
Letters	Letters show outstanding understanding of and insight into the texts and characters	Letters show good understanding of and insight into the texts and characters	Letters show limited or uneven understanding of and insight into the texts and characters	Letters show insufficient or inaccurate understanding of and insight into the texts and characters
Narrative explanation (cite relevant and sufficient textual evidence)	Narrative explanation is clear, coherent, and shows excellent insight into the texts	Narrative explanation is solid and shows good insight into the texts	Narrative explanation is limited or uneven and shows some insight into the texts	Narrative explanation is unclear and/or incoherent and shows little insight into the texts
Collaboration (initiate and participate effectively in collaboration)	Student takes responsibility for his or her own work; collaborates well with others; negotiates group dynamics well	Student takes responsibility for his or her own work; collaborates sufficiently with others; shows some success negotiating group dynamics	Student takes limited responsibility for his or her own work; collaborates minimally with others; attempts to negotiate group dynamics	Student takes no responsibility for his or her own work; student does not collaborate with others; student struggles to or is unable to negotiate group dynamics
Vocabulary (use domain-specific vocabulary)	Several "words to own" from the unit are used correctly	Some "words to own" from the unit are used correctly	One or more "words to own" from the unit are used but perhaps not correctly or effectively	No "words to own" from the unit are used
Class presentation (presentation of knowledge and ideas)	Presentation of the project is effective, concise, logical, and organized	Presentation of the project is generally but not fully effective, concise, logical, and organized	Presentation of the project is somewhat effective, but with some issues of brevity, logic, and organization	Presentation of the project is not effective, with serious problems in brevity, logic, and organization

Does Everyone Deserve a Good Lawyer?

Stephen Jones, *"The Case for Unpopular Clients"*

TEACHER'S GUIDE
Overview

In the following *Wall Street Journal* editorial from 2010, attorney Stephen Jones argues that all defendants, no matter how unpopular, including his own past client, convicted Oklahoma City bomber Timothy McVeigh, deserve fair legal representation. He also declares that attorneys should not be subject to any kind of recrimination or intimidation for doing so. Discussion of this article will give students the opportunity to consider this core principle of the U.S. judicial system, so central to *Mockingbird*, in terms of a more current issue.

Timing

This article is best used after students have read at least through chapter 11 of *Mockingbird* (when Jem and Scout face Mrs. Dubose's condemnations of Atticus for defending Tom Robinson) or have finished the book. Students could be encouraged to consider this editorial in dialogue with the arguments about Atticus outlined in the *New York Times* article "To Attack a Lawyer" (in unit 7 of this volume).

Consider the following guidelines regarding when to undertake the different activities:

Essential question for discussion and writing	Objective	Suggested timing	Rubric	Additional Research
A. How does Jones open his case in order to win the interest and attention of his readers?	Students will (SW) analyze the first two paragraphs of Jones's article in order to write an essay evaluating how he tries to win over the reader to his cause.	any time—this set of questions doesn't require any knowledge of *Mockingbird*	A	N
B. Are fearless attorneys endangered?	SW analyze the consequences Atticus, Jones, and the Guantanamo attorneys face in order to write an essay evaluating the long-term effects on the justice system if lawyers are exposed to negative consequences because of their work.	after students have completed the novel but could be used earlier in a limited way	A	N
C. Does the backlash fit the crime?	SW analyze the backlashes experienced by Atticus, Jones, and the Guantanamo attorneys in order to write an essay exploring how the political climate can contribute to the backlash against a particular crime or criminal.	after students have completed the novel but could be used after chapter 21 (when the trial verdict is read) in a limited way	A	N
D. Is Atticus ethical?	SW analyze questions of legal ethics in *Mockingbird* and in Jones's defense of McVeigh in order to write an essay evaluating the legal ethics of Atticus and Jones.	after students have completed the novel but could be used after chapter 23 (Atticus and Jem's discussion of the trial) in a limited way	A	N
E. Do bad clients deserve good lawyers?	SW research examples from history when attorneys have represented unpopular clients in order to write an essay evaluating whether bad clients deserve good attorneys.	after students have completed the novel but could be used earlier in a limited way	B	Y
Class Activity				
Defending "unpopular" clients: TV talk show debate	SW research and portray an assigned or chosen character in order to conduct a mock TV talk show debating the question: "Does everyone deserve a good lawyer?"	after chapter 9 (Scout's altercation with Cecil Jacobs) or any time later	Rubric included	Y

ALA

Notes on the Article

- The editorial begins with a brief discussion of the devastation of the 1995 Oklahoma City bombing. Students may need further help understanding the magnitude of that event, the national reaction to it, and the overwhelming negative sentiment toward McVeigh, especially given the fact that the bombing occurred prior to the September 11, 2001, attacks and was, at the time, an unprecedented terrorist event.

- Students will also need a brief explanation of the immediate context of Jones's editorial: calls on the part of Republican politicians for the disclosure of the names of any Justice Department attorneys who had previously represented suspected terrorists held at Guantanamo and suggestions that these lawyers may not be completely loyal to the United States.

- Jones makes reference to "the Right" and "the Left" in relation to the political spectrum in the U.S. Students may need a brief explanation of these terms, but teachers should not feel compelled to undertake an extensive discussion of these concepts; however, interested students should be encouraged to research this aspect of American political culture further.

- Key vocabulary: zealous, advocacy, keenly, ostracized, demagoguery, partisan, discourse, implicit, opportunistic, alleged, conspirator, espionage, reservation, presumption, adversely, subordinate

Suggested Media Links

- "The Legacy of John Adams: from Boston to Guantanamo" was the theme of the American Bar Association's 2011 Law Day celebration (www.lawday.org). The ABA's Division of Public Education website offers slideshow presentations and a guide for conducting dialogues on Adams's unpopular representation of the British soldiers involved in the Boston Massacre, which Jones references in his editorial, as well as on the Scottsboro trials and on the history of the right to counsel.

- *The Response* is a thirty-minute film produced by Street Law, Inc., that takes students behind the scenes of the Combatant Status Review Tribunals held at Guantanamo from 2004 to 2007. Viewing the film offers students the opportunity to weigh the rights of detainees against national security interests.

- Video clips of news coverage of the Oklahoma City bombing and/or Timothy McVeigh's conviction and sentencing are available on YouTube.

- Associated Press coverage from 2011 about the Guantanamo tribunals is politically neutral and available on YouTube.

VOCABULARY WARM-UP

L.9-10.4, L.9-10.5, L.9-10.6

Words to own: zealous, advocacy, keenly, ostracized, demagoguery, partisan, discourse, implicit, opportunistic, alleged, conspirator, espionage, reservation, presumption, adversely, subordinate

Section A: Use context clues. Read the following sentences and use context clues to determine the meaning of the italicized words.

1. Attorney Stephen Jones writes, "I was a draftee, not a volunteer, but I *keenly* felt the ethical responsibility of lawyers to accept such appointments." Feeling something *keenly* means what? How did Jones feel about his responsibility to accept the appointment?

2. "No matter how severe the public criticism or ostracism might be, I sought to be blind to all considerations and tried to *subordinate* my self-interests to that which was best for Mr. McVeigh, applying the skill and professionalism expected of me." By *subordinating* his "self-interests" to what "was best for Mr. McVeigh," what was the writer doing?

Section B: More context clues. Here your task is to use context clues to understand the word's meaning and to practice your context clues skills.

1. Because I had an *implicit* agreement with our neighbor, I was not in a position to argue when he paid me less than I expected for my lawn-mowing services. He violated my trust; I should have asked for the terms of our agreement in writing. *Implicit* here means
   a) trusting
   b) confidential
   c) unstated
   d) inviolable

2. Which word(s) from the sentence in question 1 best helps the reader understand the meaning of *implicit*?
   a) in writing
   b) violated
   c) less
   d) agreement

3. It was *alleged* that the football team used steroids, but the players' hard work and practice was the real reason for their success on the field. *Alleged* here means
   a) rumored
   b) accusation
   c) true
   d) judgment

4. Which word(s) from the sentence in question 3 best helps the reader understand the meaning of *alleged*?
   a) real reason
   b) football team
   c) success
   d) hard work

Section C: Use the dictionary in order to understand the uncommon meanings of these common words.

1. Jones titles his editorial "The Case for *Unpopular* Clients." He isn't using the word *unpopular* to mean not well-known or not cool. What does he mean by *unpopular*?

2. Jones states that "I had to say and do for [McVeigh, his client] zealously, without *reservation*, that which he could not do or say for himself." He is not referring to making restaurant or airline *reservations*. What does he mean by *reservation*? What does it mean to do something *without reservation*?

Section D: Use the dictionary to look up the italicized words and answer the following questions based on their definitions.

1. If a lawyer considers it her duty to provide *zealous advocacy* for her clients, what might that mean?

2. What is something your friends might *ostracize* you for doing?

3. If you said that a political candidate was practicing *demagoguery*, what would you mean?

4. If the members of the two different political parties in Congress were engaging in *partisan discourse*, would you expect them to be able to resolve their differences easily or not? Why?

5. What kind of person would you expect to act *opportunistically*? Why?

6. If someone is a *conspirator* in *espionage*, what kinds of things might he or she do?

Section E: Practice using the word correctly by choosing the correct form of the word that best fits in the blank within the following sentences.

1. Although he has not been officially nominated yet, the former Massachusetts governor is the _____ Republican nominee for president.
   a) presumption
   b) presumedly
   c) presumptive
   d) presume

2. People who are allergic to certain foods can have a very serious _____ reaction if they are exposed to them.
   a) adversely
   b) adverse
   c) adversary
   d) adversity

3. My best friend and I trust each other _____; we automatically know that we will always have each other's back.
   a) implicitly
   b) implicit
   c) implicitness
   d) implicity

4. The suspect _____ kidnapped the boy and demanded a $1 million ransom from his parents, but the prosecutor has yet to actually make the case.
   a) alleged
   b) allegation
   c) alleges
   d) allegedly

Section F: Vocabulary skits. Use the model sentences and definitions to understand the words in question. Create a skit in which you address the given topic. Every member of the group must use the vocabulary word at least once during your performance of the skit.

1. *adversary*—opponent in contest, debate, or conflict
   - He was my *adversary* in the school debate, but in real life he is my best friend.
   - Teenagers sometimes feel that their parents are their *adversaries*; conflict can be a regular part of the teenager/parent relationship.
   - You can catch more bees with honey; *adversarial* relationships with others do not always produce the best results.

   Scenario: Create a skit in which some teenagers discuss whether or not they feel their parents are unnecessarily *adversarial*.

2. *discourse*—serious piece of writing or speech, serious conversation or discussion, kind of language (political discourse or literary discourse)
   - The political *discourse* used by our leaders in Congress can be partisan, high-tempered, and combative.
   - It's time we had some serious *discourse* about your future; your good grades and fine work habits suggest that you have a successful future ahead of you.
   - The students objected to the school's policy and responded with responsible *discourse* on the subject that could not be ignored by the administration.

   Scenario: Create a skit in which some workers discuss the fact that they think the company management where they work has not taken their *discourse* about workers' rights seriously.

3. *zealous*—enthusiastic, passionate, keen
   - I am *zealous* in my concerns about childhood obesity; I think no issue is more important in America today.
   - My parents find my *zealousness* for music mystifying, but I love the bands I follow.
   - The teacher wished her students were as *zealous* about their homework as they were about video games.

   Scenario: Create a skit in which some gun control advocates discuss why this is the time to be *zealous* in the pursuit of new laws regulating guns and ammunition.

ESSENTIAL QUESTION: DOES EVERYONE DESERVE A GOOD LAWYER?
Introduction

Just as Atticus Finch defies public opinion in Maycomb when he agrees to represent Tom Robinson in *To Kill a Mockingbird*, U.S. attorneys have defended in court politically unpopular suspected terrorists held at the U.S. military base at Guantanamo and have experienced opposition and threats similar to what Atticus faces. In this editorial, attorney Stephen Jones, who represented the Oklahoma City bomber, Timothy McVeigh, in the 1990s, explains why lawyers must take on controversial clients.

Reflect on the essential question: What does the question suggest to you? What current conflicts does the question make you think of? What do you think the article will be about?

Reflect on the introduction: The introduction tells you that the piece you are about to read is an editorial written by attorney Stephen Jones. What is an editorial and why do people write them? What connection does there seem to be between him and Atticus? How do you think Jones's experience as a lawyer will influence the way he writes his editorial?

Reflect on the title: "The Case for Unpopular Clients." What does the phrase mean to you? How does it introduce what Jones is writing about?

Jones wrote this editorial in 2010, after Republican politicians called for the disclosure of the names of any Justice Department attorneys who had previously represented suspected terrorists held at Guantanamo and suggested that these lawyers may not be completely loyal to the United States.

The Case for Unpopular Clients
By Stephen Jones

In 1995, Timothy McVeigh was charged with committing the largest act of terrorism on American soil: the bombing of the Alfred P. Murrah Federal Building in Oklahoma City. This tragic act resulted in 168 deaths, including those of 19 children under the age of 6 and 8 federal law-enforcement agents. More than 500 people were seriously injured, 200 buildings had to be leveled because of structural damage, the skyline of Oklahoma City was instantly changed and the uninsured economic losses were estimated at $800 million.

Federal judges in Oklahoma City asked me to accept the appointment as Mr. McVeigh's lead defense counsel in his federal trial. I agreed. I was a draftee, not a volunteer, but I *keenly* felt the ethical responsibility of lawyers to accept such appointments. To me, it was important in a period of growing domestic unrest and violence to demonstrate that Mr. McVeigh could receive a fair trial and *zealous advocacy* within the framework of a civilian trial under the Federal Rules of Evidence, the Federal Rules of Criminal Procedure and the United States Constitution.

For this representation, I was demonized, *ostracized* and exposed to physical and economic risks. The FBI investigated threats against my life, and I had no less than half a dozen serious security incidents at my home. I placed a loaded revolver in my office desk drawer and a loaded shotgun in my closet at home. Because of threats, another lawyer on the defense team was authorized to carry a concealed weapon. My family had armed guards on our property for 2½ years, motion detectors, electronic eyes, unlisted telephone numbers and emergency-response numbers. A law practice of 25 years was destroyed. It took me seven years to build it back to pre-1995 levels.

> **Notice** Jones's explanation of how he became Timothy McVeigh's lawyer. Why do you think he feels the need to explain that he was appointed?
>
> **Vocabulary:** Jones writes that "it was important . . . to demonstrate that Mr. McVeigh could receive a fair trial and zealous advocacy within the framework of a civilian trial." What is he saying? What does "zealous advocacy" mean? Put this into your own words.

More recently, Liz Cheney, William Kristol and Keep America Safe pressed their demands to the Department of Justice for the public identification of lawyers who, while in private practice and prior to their appointments at the department, either represented Guantanamo detainees or argued for changes in the legal policy concerning detainees. Their demands escalated to *demagoguery*, with the lawyers branded as the "al Qaeda Seven," as though attorneys who represent detainees are members of al Qaeda.

On one level, it is easy to see what these attacks are: *partisan* politics at the outer limits of generally accepted political *discourse*. At a more fundamental level, Ms. Cheney and others are making fearless lawyers an endangered species in this country.

There are already too many timid lawyers now, and some lawyers willing to take up controversial cases do it because of an angle to the case which furthers a political cause, whether on the right or the left.

> **Key idea:** Jones is comparing what he experienced while defending Timothy McVeigh in the 1990s to the current situation facing lawyers defending Guantanamo detainees. What might happen if these Guantanamo lawyers were publicly identified? How is this situation similar to Jones's experience and what Atticus faces?
>
> **Vocabulary:** Jones says, "Their demands escalated to demagoguery, with the lawyers branded as the 'al Qaeda Seven,' as though attorneys who represent detainees are members of al Qaeda." What is he saying here? Put this into your own words. What is he objecting to?
>
> **Key idea:** Jones writes that "Ms. Cheney and others are making fearless lawyers an endangered species in this country." What does he mean? What is he concerned about?

Implicit in the *opportunistic* demand for the release of the lawyers' identities is the assumption that they cannot now fairly represent the Department of Justice and their country, and that somehow they are unpatriotic allies of terrorists.

To carry that argument to its logical extension, President John Adams should not have signed the Declaration of Independence, or even become president, because he defended British Redcoats who were charged with the murder of colonists in the Boston Massacre. One of the most distinguished federal judges in the country's history, Harold Medina would have been disqualified from appointment because during World War II he accepted an appointment to represent Anthony Cramer, a naturalized American citizen and *alleged* co-*conspirator* with German saboteurs, on a charge of treason. Kenneth C. Royall also could not have served as secretary of war and later as the first secretary of the Army because he, too, represented alleged Nazi saboteurs charged before a military commission with *espionage*. U.S. Sen. Reverdy Johnson would have been expelled for defending Mary Surratt, charged as a conspirator in the assassination of President Abraham Lincoln.

Neither logic nor experience nor history demonstrates that the points being made by Ms. Cheney and her allies have any merit. They represent forensic vigilantism, a political lynch-mob mentality.

Lawyers are required by their code of ethics to accept judicial appointments to represent defendants even when the defendant is charged with mass murder, or may be a member—or even a ringleader—of a terrorist organization.

Equally, lawyers have an ethical obligation to represent individuals who represent unpopular or controversial positions.

> **Vocabulary:** Jones says that "Implicit in the opportunistic demand for the release of the lawyers' identities is the assumption that they cannot now fairly represent the Department of Justice and their country. . . ." What is he saying here? Put this into your own words.
>
> **Notice** that Jones lists several examples here. What purpose do these examples serve? What do you notice about the kinds of examples Jones uses? How do these examples support Jones's argument?

> **Vocabulary:** Jones writes that the accusations being made by "Ms. Cheney and her allies . . . represent forensic vigilantism, a political lynch-mob mentality." What is Jones saying here? Put this into your own words.
>
> **Key idea:** Jones refers to his ethical obligations in accepting his appointment to defend Timothy McVeigh. What are ethics? Why would it have been a matter of ethics for Jones to accept his appointment to defend McVeigh?

When I took on Mr. McVeigh's case, in addition to my ethical commitments, I thought it was important that Mr. McVeigh be represented by an Oklahoma trial lawyer. As I viewed my oath of obligation as a lawyer, I had a duty to accept, and once I accepted, it was my duty to see that the legal system established by our Constitution worked, that nothing was taken from Mr. McVeigh, neither his life nor his liberty, except by due process of law. I had to say and do for him zealously, without *reservation*, that which he could not do or say for himself.

There were restless nights in which I had recurring dreams of either someone parking a Ryder truck outside my home and blowing it up or my being assassinated in the hallway outside my office.

My position as Mr. McVeigh's defense counsel was a nearly impossible one, in which I could not possibly satisfy everyone. Ultimately, I decided I could satisfy only my professional conscience. I sought to accomplish this in the face of an overwhelming public condemnation, a demonization of Mr. McVeigh in which the *presumption* of innocence had been replaced by the assumption of guilt, and accomplish it in a community where literally thousands, if not tens of thousands, of lives had been *adversely* affected, indeed ruined, by the act with which he was charged.

> **Vocabulary:** Jones refers to "due process of law." What does this term mean and what is Jones saying here? Put this into your own words.
>
> **Notice** that Jones says his "position as Mr. McVeigh's defense counsel was a nearly impossible one, in which I could not possibly satisfy everyone. Ultimately, I decided I could satisfy only my professional conscience." Compare Jones's feelings about McVeigh's case with Atticus's feelings about representing Tom Robinson.

No matter how severe the public criticism or *ostracism* might be, I sought to be blind to all considerations and tried to *subordinate* my self-interests to that which was best for Mr. McVeigh, applying the skill and professionalism expected of me. I could not do it with one arm tied behind my back.

Because we have rejected in this country a private system of vengeance for an institutionalized judicial process, courts must rely upon the experience and integrity of defense counsel. These lawyers have to be willing to accept the

> **Key idea:** Jones notes that "we have rejected in this country a private system of vengeance for an institutionalized judicial process." What does he mean?

challenge. That necessary reliance is damaged by the short-sighted and ill-advised attacks now being made on the Justice Department lawyers.

Many lawyers in private practice represent clients, interests and
points of view that are not their
own personal views, or the views
of later clients, including governments they may work for. Three
principles protect the public interests, the lawyer and the rule of law.

> **Consider** the three principles Jones
> describes. Summarize them in your own
> words. Why are they so important to our
> justice system? What could happen if we
> didn't have these principles?

Those principles are: the principle of partisanship—the adversarial system in which
each side presents its best evidence to an impartial tribunal; the principle of neutrality;
and the principle of nonaccountability. The principle of neutrality purports to exempt
lawyers from the normal moral practice of judging someone to have acted immorally
if they have knowingly and deliberately helped another to act immorally. According to
the principle, a lawyer is not to be judged by the moral status of their clients. The principle of nonaccountability follows: We cannot properly assume these lawyers identify
or sympathize with their clients' goals. Lawyers must remain professionally neutral
with respect to the moral merits of their clients or their clients' objectives. The lawyers
must not allow their own views to affect the diligence or *zealousness* with which they
pursue their clients' lawful objectives.

The criticism and shrill *demagoguery* of Keep America Safe would denigrate not
only these principles but fundamentally undermine due process of law. These partisan
attacks are misplaced, gratuitous and weaken our democratic ideals. The identities of
the lawyers are sought to embarrass and demonize them personally and professionally,
to try to dishonor them. It is an effort to intimidate other lawyers from honoring their
professional responsibility.

The day when scare mongers can intimidate lawyers into not doing their jobs is a
day in which liberty is threatened. The justice of a society is measured not by how it
treats its best, but how it treats its worst.

All lawyers should stand firm and
reject the unwarranted insinuation
that the Department of Justice lawyers are unpatriotic allies of terrorists, or that their past cases will
shade their responsibilities in their

> **Notice** how Jones concludes his editorial.
> Whom is he specifically addressing? Why
> does he conclude his editorial this way?

current positions. The same goes for Republicans such as myself who value the traditions
of our party and who remember that the first elected Republican president himself, Abraham Lincoln, defended unpopular causes and clients, even those accused of murder.

Jones, Stephen. "The Case for Unpopular Clients." Editorial. *Wsj.com*. Wall Street
Journal, Dow Jones & Company, 13 Mar. 2010. Web. 3 Feb. 2014.

CHECK FOR UNDERSTANDING   RI.9-10.1, RI.9-10.4, RI.9-10.5, RI.9-10.6

1. In the article, Jones says that for representing Timothy McVeigh, he "was demonized, *ostracized* and exposed to physical and economic risks." By *ostracized* he means
   a) fired
   b) excluded
   c) defended
   d) terrified

2. In his editorial, Jones writes that, "Ms. Cheney and others are making fearless lawyers an endangered species in this country." What is he concerned about?
   a) That lawyers are defending clients who don't deserve representation.
   b) That fewer lawyers are willing to defend unpopular clients because of threats.
   c) That lawyers are putting themselves in danger to defend unpopular clients.
   d) That lawyers are breaking the law in defending unpopular clients.

3. Jones says, "*Implicit* in the opportunistic demand for the release of the lawyers'
   identities is the assumption that they cannot now fairly represent the Department
   of Justice and their country." By *implicit*, Jones means
   a) insincere
   b) stated
   c) selfish
   d) unspoken

4. Which of the following is NOT one of the explanations Jones offers for why he had
   a duty to represent Timothy McVeigh?
   a) He had an ethical obligation to represent even unpopular clients.
   b) His legal experience made him the best person to defend McVeigh.
   c) He wanted to make sure McVeigh received a good defense.
   d) He thought McVeigh should have an attorney from Oklahoma.

5. According to Jones, Keep America Safe's calls to publicly identify lawyers who have
   defended Guantanamo detainees are a threat to "due process of law" that could
   "weaken our democratic ideals" because identifying the attorneys
   a) could help other suspected terrorists find good lawyers.
   b) could leave other unpopular clients without legal representation.
   c) could delay the trials of the detainees still held at Guantanamo.
   d) would turn the lawyers into celebrities and distract them from their duties.

WRITING AND DISCUSSION

RI.9-10.1, RI.9-10.4, RI.9-10.5, RI.9-10.6, W.9-10.2, W.9-10.4, W.9-10.5, W.9-10.9, SL.9-10.1, L.9-10.1, L.9-10.2, L.9-10.3, L.9-10.5

ALA

A. How does Jones open his case in order to win the interest and attention of his readers?

1. **Discuss:** Jones begins his editorial with dramatic facts and statistics about the Oklahoma City bombing. Why do you think he does that? How does the language he uses support this purpose? What effect do his rhetorical choices have on the reader? *Use Table A-1 to identify and analyze the facts Jones uses and the effects they have on readers.*

2. **Discuss:** In his second paragraph, Jones explains how he became Timothy McVeigh's attorney. What effect does this information have on the reader? How does it impact Jones's overall argument? *Use Table A-2 to identify and analyze the information Jones offers and its impacts on the reader and his argument.*

3. **Write:** Consider the opening of Jones's article. How does he try to win over the reader to his cause in the first two paragraphs? *Use evidence from the article in your response.*

ALA

Table A-1: Facts about the Oklahoma City Bombing

Facts about Oklahoma City bombing	Rhetorical choice/language use	What Jones is trying to convey to the reader
"This tragic act resulted in 168 deaths, including those of 19 children under the age of 6 and eight federal law-enforcement agents."	Jones emphasizes the large number of deaths and the deaths of small children. He also notes that the adult victims included those dedicated to protecting others.	The bombing killed many children as well as innocent and honorable people and was a terrible act of violence.

Table A-2: How Jones Came to Represent Timothy McVeigh

How Jones became McVeigh's attorney	What Jones is trying to convey to the reader	Implication for argument
"Federal judges in Oklahoma City asked me to accept the appointment as Mr. McVeigh's lead defense counsel in his federal trial."	He was appointed as McVeigh's attorney by federal judges.	Important people asked Jones to take the assignment; he is presenting himself as politically neutral and willing to do his professional duty.

B. Are fearless attorneys endangered?

RL.9-10.1, RL.9-10.2, RL.9-10.3, RI.9-10.1, RI.9-10.2, RI.9-10.3, RI.9-10.5, RI.9-10.6, W.9-10.1, W.9-10.4, W.9-10.5, W.9-10.9, SL.9-10.1, L.9-10.1, L.9-10.2, L.9-10.3, L.9-10.6

1. **Discuss:** Jones argues that lawyers who represented detainees held at Guantanamo should not be publicly identified because of the negative consequences they could face. Consider the different consequences Atticus, Jones, and the Guantanamo attorneys face because of their work. *Use Table B-1 to identify and compare those consequences.*

2. **Discuss:** Jones says the attacks by "Ms. Cheney and others are making fearless lawyers an endangered species in this country." Do you agree with Jones? Do you think the kinds of attacks Atticus, Jones, and the Guantanamo lawyers faced threaten to make "fearless lawyers" an "endangered species"? If you were a lawyer asked to represent the Guantanamo detainees, how would Cheney's attacks make you feel? Would exposure make you reluctant to continue your work on behalf of the detainees?

3. **Write:** What might the long-term effects be on the justice system if lawyers were exposed to personal danger and political and professional backlash because of their work? *Use evidence from* Mockingbird *and Jones's editorial in your response.*

Table B-1: Consequences Attorneys Face

Attorney	Example of consequence	Discussion
Stephen Jones	"I was demonized, ostracized and exposed to physical and economic risks. The FBI investigated threats against my life, and I had no less than a dozen serious security incidents at my home. . . . My family had armed guards on our property for 2½ years, motion detectors, electronic eyes, unlisted telephone numbers and emergency-response numbers. A law practice of 25 years was destroyed. It took me seven years to build it back to pre-1995 levels."	Jones faces harassment, danger to himself and his family and serious financial damage to his law business.
Atticus Finch		
Guantanamo attorneys		

C. Does the backlash fit the crime?

RL.9-10.1, RL.9-10.2, RL.9-10.3, RI.9-10.1,
RI.9-10.2, RI.9-10.3, RI.9-10.5, RI.9-10.6,
W.9-10.1, W.9-10.4, W.9-10.5, W.9-10.9,
SL.9-10.1, L.9-10.1, L.9-10.2, L.9-10.3

1. **Discuss:** According to merriam-webster.com, a backlash is "a sudden violent backward movement or reaction" or "a strong adverse reaction (as to a recent political or social development)." For example, teen suicides linked to cyberbullying have caused a backlash against Facebook and other social networks. Can you think of another example of a recent backlash in which an event or movement caused a strong public reaction?

2. **Discuss:** The clients that Atticus, Jones, and the Guantanamo lawyers defended were hated because of their alleged crimes, but the lawyers all got caught up in the backlash against their clients. What issues and emotions were stirred up in each of these situations? *Use Table C-1 to identify the characteristics of the political/social climate and reasons the attorneys were attacked in each case.*

3. **Write**: Does the backlash always fit the crime? Answer this question by discussing how in each of these situations the lawyers were caught up in the backlash against their clients. What underlying concerns were people expressing by attacking Atticus, Jones, and the Guantanamo lawyers? What issues did each of these cases stir up? *Use evidence from* Mockingbird *and Jones's editorial in your response.*

Table C-1: Reasons Attorneys Were Attacked

Lawyer	Client	Alleged crime	Political/social climate	Reasons for attacks on attorneys
Jones	Timothy McVeigh	Bombing a federal building in Oklahoma City	Intense horror at an act of terrorism being carried out in the U.S. and the massive destruction and loss of life it caused	People hated McVeigh so much they felt he didn't deserve a defense
Atticus				
Guantanamo attorneys				

D. Is Atticus ethical?

RL.9-10.1, RL.9-10.2, RL.9-10.3, RI.9-10.1, RI.9-10.2, RI.9-10.3, RI.9-10.5, RI.9-10.6, W.9-10.1, W.9-10.4, W.9-10.5, W.9-10.9, SL.9-10.1, L.9-10.1, L.9-10.2, L.9-10.3, L.9-10.6

1. **Discuss:** What are ethics? What does it mean to follow a code of ethics? Why are ethics important and what is their purpose in society?
2. **Discuss:** Consider the issue of legal ethics. Jones writes:

   Lawyers are required by their code of ethics to accept judicial appointments to represent defendants even when the defendant is charged with mass murder, or may be a member—or even a ringleader—of a terrorist organization. Equally, lawyers have an ethical obligation to represent individuals who represent unpopular or controversial positions.

   Why would it be unethical for a lawyer to refuse to represent a client based on political or social controversy? What might happen if lawyers like Jones refused to represent clients such as McVeigh or the Guantanamo detainees? Does it make a difference whether the lawyer thinks the client is innocent or guilty?
3. **Discuss:** Compare Jones's explanation of why he defended McVeigh with Atticus's explanation for why he defends Tom Robinson. *Use Figure D-1 below to identify the similarities and differences between the two explanations.*
4. **Write:** Given that Atticus defends a client he thinks is innocent, while Jones defended a client he believed to be guilty, whom do you find more ethical, Atticus or Jones? Why? *Use evidence from* Mockingbird *and Jones's editorial in your response.*

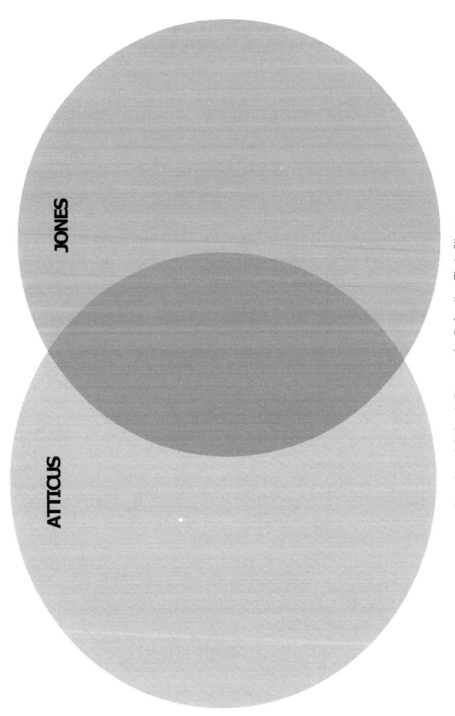

JONES

ATTICUS

Jones's and Atticus's Reasons for Defending Their Clients

E. Do bad clients deserve good lawyers?

RL.9-10.1, RL.9-10.2, RL.9-10.3, RI.9-10.1, RI.9-10.2, RI.9-10.3, W.9-10.1, W.9-10.4, W.9-10.5, W.9-10.7, W.9-10.8, W.9-10.9, SL.9-10.1, L.9-10.1, L.9-10.2, L.9-10.3, L.9-10.6

1. **Research:** Jones gives several examples from American history of lawyers who defended notorious clients. Use the Internet to research two or more of these examples. Who were these clients? What did they do? Why would it have been unpopular for a lawyer to represent them? *Use Table E-1 to collect and organize your research.*

2. **Discuss:** Miss Maudie says: "The justice of a society is measured not by how it treats its best, but how it treats its worst." What do you think she means by this statement? What does she mean by "worst"? By this measure, how just is the society of *Mockingbird*? *Use Table E-2 to identify and analyze how certain characters in Mockingbird are treated.*

3. **Write:** Should lawyers defend bad, unpopular, or politically notorious clients? Does everyone deserve a good lawyer? Why or why not? *Use evidence from Jones's editorial and Mockingbird in your response.*

Table E-1: Lawyers Who Defended Notorious Clients

Lawyer	Client	Alleged crime	Reason for unpopularity
Stephen Jones	Timothy McVeigh	Bombing a federal building in Oklahoma City	People hated McVeigh so much they felt he didn't deserve a defense

Table E-2: How the "Worst" Are Treated in *Mockingbird*

Person	How he or she is among Maycomb's "worst"	How treated
Tom Robinson	A somewhat crippled black man	Tom Robinson is falsely accused by Mayella; unjustly convicted by the Maycomb jury; and then killed in prison.
Bob Ewell		

CLASS ACTIVITY

RL.9-10.1, RL.9-10.3, RI.9-10.1, RI-10.9.2, RI.9-10.3, RI.9-10.5, RI.9-10.6, W.9-10.1, W.9-10.2, W.9-10.3, W.9-10.4, W.9-10.5, W.9-10.6, W.9-10.7, W.9-10.8, W.9-10.9, SL.9-10.1, SL.9-10.2, SL.9-10.3, SL.9-10.4, SL.9-10.5, SL.9-10.6, L.9-10.1, L.9-10.2, L.9-10.3, L.9-10.5, L.9-10.6

Task: Your goal is to conduct a TV talk show debating the question: "Does everyone deserve a good lawyer?" Each student will be required to determine (based on research and/or understanding of the novel) how his or her assigned character would act and speak during such a debate.

Talk show host or cohosts:

- Prepares questions for both panelists and audience members.
- Acts as moderator for the debate, asking questions of the panelists and audience members and promoting balanced and civil discussion among all parties.

Panelists:

- Atticus Finch
- Judge Taylor
- Tom Robinson
- Stephen Jones
- Timothy McVeigh
- Guantanamo detainee
- Guantanamo lawyer
- Lynne Cheney

Audience members:

- Miss Maudie
- Heck Tate
- Calpurnia
- Dolphus Raymond
- Aunt Alexandra
- Walter Cunningham
- Other members of lynch mob
- Supporters of Lynne Cheney and Keep America Safe

In addition, each student must produce the following:

1. **Explanation of character:** Write a narrative in which you explain how you went about determining how your character would act, what he or she would say during the debate in response to particular questions, and how he or she would perceive and react to the other characters. Justify (with textual evidence) how your character's words and actions make sense based on your research and/or your understanding of *Mockingbird*.
2. **Postdebate evaluation:** (1) Write a narrative in which you evaluate how the talk show debate was conducted. Discuss how well your classmates represented their characters: did their words and actions make sense for their roles? (2) Reflecting on specific evidence from the debate, Jones's editorial, *Mockingbird*, your own research, as well as the exchange of ideas during the debate, discuss the essential question: "Does everyone deserve a good lawyer?" Has your position changed in any way? Why or why not?

CLASS ACTIVITY RUBRIC

Category	4—Excellent	3—Good	2—Satisfactory	1—Unsatisfactory
Performance of role/ character (presentation of knowledge and ideas)	Performance demonstrates strong and insightful comprehension of character through ample, effective reference to evidence from research and novel	Performance demonstrates solid comprehension of character through frequent, effective reference to evidence from research and novel	Performance demonstrates some comprehension of character through occasional, though perhaps vague or ineffective, reference to evidence from research and novel	Performance does not demonstrate comprehension of character through reference to evidence from research and novel
Collaboration (initiate and participate effectively in conversation and collaboration)	Student participates clearly and persuasively in debate	Student participates somewhat clearly and persuasively in debate	Student participates somewhat clearly but perhaps not persuasively in debate	Student does not participate clearly or persuasively in debate
Explanation of character (cite relevant and sufficient textual evidence)	Narrative demonstrates strong and insightful comprehension of character through ample, effective reference to evidence from research and novel	Narrative demonstrates solid comprehension of character through frequent, effective reference to evidence from research and novel	Narrative demonstrates some comprehension of character through occasional, though perhaps vague or ineffective, reference to evidence from research and novel	Narrative does not demonstrate comprehension of character through reference to evidence from research and novel
Debate evaluation and reflection (cite relevant and sufficient textual evidence)	Evaluation and reflection make clear, insightful arguments based on substantial, specific evidence from debate and texts	Evaluation and reflection make clear arguments based on specific evidence from debate and texts	Evaluation and reflection make arguments that may be vague or not clearly based on evidence from debate and texts	Evaluation and reflection do not make arguments based on evidence from debate and texts
Vocabulary (use domain-specific vocabulary)	Several "words to own" from the unit are used correctly in debate and/or narratives	Some "words to own" from the unit are used correctly in debate and/or narratives	One or more "words to own" from the unit are used but perhaps not correctly or effectively	No "words to own" from the unit are used in debate and/or narratives
Documentation (in-text citation and works cited)	Essay(s) conform to the appropriate style guidelines (MLA) for in-text citation and works cited	Essay(s) conform with limited errors to the appropriate style guidelines (MLA) for in-text citation and works cited	Essay(s) attempt to conform to the appropriate style guidelines (MLA) for in-text citation and works cited but do so ineffectively or inaccurately	Essay(s) do not conform to the appropriate style guidelines (MLA) for in-text citation and works cited

What Is a Lynch Mob?

Clarence Norris and Sybil D. Washington,
The Last of the Scottsboro Boys:
An Autobiography, *and Haywood
Patterson and Earl Conrad,*
Scottsboro Boy

TEACHER'S GUIDE
Overview

After the Civil War and through and beyond the Civil Rights Movement, lynching was an extrajudicial form of political terrorism, used particularly against African American men and women who challenged white political dominance. According to figures from the Tuskegee Institute, between 1882 and 1951, 3,437 African American and 1,294 white men and women were lynched in the United States. Lynchings were carried out by hanging or shooting but also included castration, dismemberment, and other methods of torture. Lynchings were often but not always justified by accusations, particularly accusations of rape, against lynching victims. Lynchings were sometimes community events, in which men, women, and children, often with the tacit consent of law enforcement, gathered together to participate. An exhibit at the New York Historical Society in 2000 displayed postcards and other souvenirs that once circulated as popular mementos of lynchings.

In chapter 15, Scout, Jem, and Dill come upon and prevent the lynching of Tom Robinson by a small mob that includes Walter Cunningham. To place this incident into a broader context for students, we have selected excerpts from the autobiographies of two of the Scottsboro Boys, a group of nine black teenagers, aged thirteen to nineteen, accused in March 1931 of raping two white women on board a train in

Alabama. The Scottsboro case attracted international attention as the young men were repeatedly tried, retried, and sentenced to death for the assault, despite a lack of physical evidence and the fact that one of the supposed victims recanted; the case was one of the singular events to shape *To Kill a Mockingbird*. The excerpts describe two attempts to lynch the young men, first when they were removed from the train and second, shortly after, as they awaited trial in a jail in Scottsboro, Alabama. The last three of the Scottsboro Boys to still have convictions from the case on their records, including Haywood Patterson, were officially pardoned by the state of Alabama in April 2013.

Timing

These excerpts can be used in relation to chapter 15 in *Mockingbird* where Scout prevents the lynching of Tom Robinson or after the family's discussion about the incident at the beginning of chapter 16. But the selection might also be read at any time to set up the larger political context for the novel.

Consider the following guidelines regarding when to undertake the different activities:

Essential question for discussion and writing	Objective	Suggested timing	Suggested rubric	Additional research
A. How did it feel to be a Scottsboro Boy?	Students will (SW) analyze Norris's and Patterson's use of language in order to explore their attempts to shape their readers' understanding of how it felt to be a Scottsboro Boy.	any time—this set of questions doesn't require any knowledge of *Mockingbird*	A	N
B. What was a lynch mob like?	SW compare and analyze the descriptions of lynch mobs in the two Scottsboro texts and in *Mockingbird*.	after chapter 15 (when the mob tries to lynch Tom Robinson) and the beginning of chapter 16 (when the family discusses the incident)	A	N
C. Is the Klan really gone, Atticus?	SW research the KKK and analyze the discussion of the KKK within *Mockingbird* in order to evaluate Atticus's sentiments about the Klan.	after chapter 15 (when the mob tries to lynch Tom Robinson) and the beginning of chapter 16 (when the family discusses the incident)	B	Y

Essential question for discussion and writing	Objective	Suggested timing	Suggested rubric	Additional research
Class Activity				
Reporting on the Scottsboro Boys and the Maycomb lynch mob	SW research news coverage of the Scottsboro Boys and write news articles about the Scottsboro Boys and about the Maycomb lynch mob for the *Maycomb Tribune* as Mr. Underwood.	after chapter 25 (when Mr. Underwood writes his editorial about Tom Robinson's death in prison)	Rubric included	Y

Notes on the Article

- These selections offer a crucial piece of context to introduce the Scottsboro case to students, which was a crucial context for *Mockingbird*.
- The language and content of the excerpts and in some of the suggested media links are startling and disturbing. They underline the brutality that Scout elides in her narration of the episode with Tom Robinson. Teachers will need to proceed with care and caution.
- The vocabulary in these excerpts is generally accessible.
- Key vocabulary: lynching, mob, bayonet, irons, credit, dusk, extrajudicial

Suggested Media Links

- PBS's *Scottsboro: An American Tragedy*—available on YouTube and DVD
- *The Scottsboro Boys Trials* documentary—available on YouTube
- Discussion of the Scottsboro case and of lynching by Emory University professor Carol Anderson—short lecture-style videos available online
- Musarium: *Without Sanctuary: Lynching Photography in America*—photos, essays, a film, and a wide variety of documents available online
- Billie Holiday's song about lynching, "Strange Fruit"—available on YouTube

VOCABULARY WARM-UP   L.9-10.4, L.9-10.5, L.9-10.6

> **Words to own**: lynching, mob, bayonet, irons, credit, dusk, extrajudicial

Section A: Use context clues. Read the following sentences and use context clues to determine the meaning of the italicized words.

1. Clarence Norris writes that a guard "struck out at me with his *bayonet*" and "slashed my right hand open to the bone." Based on the context here, what do you think a *bayonet* is? Was that the right thing for a guard to have done to Norris?

2. Norris writes of seeing the railroad tracks "lined with a *mob* of men," a "sea of white faces, screaming." Based on the context in which it is used, do you think the *mob* has good or bad intentions toward the Scottsboro boys? Why or why not? Do you ever use the word *mob* to describe a group with good intentions?

Section B: More context clues. Here your task is to use context clues to understand the word's meaning and to practice your context clues skills.

1. The introduction to this section's readings explains that *lynching* was an extrajudicial form of political terrorism, used particularly against African American men and women who challenged white political dominance. *Lynching* here means
   a) political speech
   b) execution
   c) justice
   d) terror

2. Which word from the sentence in question 1 best helps the reader understand the meaning of *lynching*?
   a) men
   b) form
   c) terrorism
   d) white

May be photocopied for classroom use. *Using Informational Text to Teach* To Kill a Mockingbird by Audrey Fisch and Susan Chenelle © 2014 (Lanham, MD: Rowman & Littlefield).

3. In this same sentence, if you know that "extra" as a prefix means outside of, you can determine that extrajudicial means
   a) inside the justice system
   b) from the justice system
   c) outside the justice system
   d) outside of politics

Section C: Use the dictionary in order to understand the uncommon meanings of these common words.

1. Patterson describes how the deputies handcuffed the boys separately and how he "didn't want for them to put those *irons* on." Here, he isn't talking about the deputies ironing wrinkles out of shirts. What are the *irons* he doesn't want put on? Why do you think the word "irons" here is similar to the word for the instrument we use to remove wrinkles from clothing?

2. Patterson describes the deputies "taking some kind of funny *credit* for turning us over." He doesn't mean *credit* in the sense of the ability to borrow money or use a credit card. What does he mean? What kind of *credit* would the deputies get for turning the boys over to the crowd? Who would give them this *credit*?

Section D: Use the dictionary to look up the italicized words and answer the following questions based on their definitions.

1. If people gather around *dusk*, would you expect it to be easy or hard to see? Why?

2. If a politician argues for the need for *extrajudicial* justice, would you consider him to be a good advocate for his government or someone who is undermining the government? Why? Are there ever exceptions?

3. Supreme Court Justice Clarence Thomas was famous for accusing the Senate Judiciary Committee of conducting a high-tech *lynching* at his confirmation hearing. What did he mean? Do you agree with his use of the term *lynching* in this context?

Section E: Practice parts of speech by choosing the correct word that best fits in the blank within the following sentences.

1. The principal often talks about how the students are a _____ to the school; she is proud of our achievements and think they reflect well on her and the school.
   a) creditor
   b) credits
   c) credit
   d) creditable

2. One of the ugly pieces of our nation's history is the reality of _____ mobs who kidnapped people from their homes and tortured and killed them in the name of extrajudicial justice.
   a) lynching
   b) lynchs
   c) lynches
   d) lynch

Section F: Vocabulary skits. Use the model sentences and definitions to understand the words in question. Create a skit in which you address the given topic. Every member of the group must use the vocabulary word at least once during your performance of the skit.

1. *extrajudicial*—outside the justice system
   ▪ He spoke about the need for *extrajudicial* justice because of the corruption of the courts.
   ▪ When the justice system doesn't function, citizens often turn to *extrajudicial* justice.
   ▪ The lynch mob decided to enact its own *extrajudicial* punishment on the man, but history later revealed that he was innocent of the crime.

   Scenario: Create a skit in which some students discuss whether or not the best way to deal with school bullies would be to create a student-centered, *extrajudicial* system of punishment. Other students argue that school officials should be involved and that the students should not take the law into their own hands when dealing with these bullies, no matter how bad their behavior has been.

2. *mob*—a gang or out-of-control mass of people, often intent on violence
   - We often talk about a *mob* scene at the mall or at a concert, but *mobs* have traditionally been sinister.
   - After the Supreme Court's controversial decision, a *mob* gathered on the National Mall in Washington, DC, but politicians were able to turn a moment of tension into an opportunity for reflection, debate, and political action.
   - The principal accused the students of forming a *mob* in her office, but the students simply wanted to gather together and voice their objections about the new school lunch rules.

   Scenario: Create a skit in which a political dictator and his secret police react to the news that a *mob* has gathered outside his presidential palace. The *mob* is led by a charismatic young leader who voices the group's concerns about low wages, food insecurity, and pollution. How do the dictator and his police force plan to react to the *mob* and its leader?

ESSENTIAL QUESTION:
WHAT IS A LYNCH MOB?
Introduction

After the Civil War, *lynching* was an *extrajudicial* form of political terrorism, used particularly against African American men and women who challenged white political dominance. According to figures from the Tuskegee Institute, between 1882 and 1951, 3,437 African American and 1,294 white men and women were lynched in the United States. Lynchings were carried out by hanging or shoot-

Reflect on the essential question: What does the question suggest to you? What does the word "mob" make you think about? What do you know about lynching?

Reflect on the introduction: The introduction gives you a brief history of lynching in the United States. What did you know about lynching before reading this? Is there anything in this introduction that particularly surprises you about lynching?

Research: What is the Tuskegee Institute? What kind of work does the institute do today?

ing, but also included castration, dismemberment, and other methods of torture. Lynchings were often but not always justified by accusations, particularly accusations of rape, against lynching victims. Lynchings were sometimes community events, in which men, women, and children, often with the tacit consent of law enforcement, gathered together to participate. An exhibit at the New York Historical Society in 2000 displayed postcards and other souvenirs that once circulated as popular mementos of lynchings.

In 1931, in a case that attracted international attention and was instrumental in shaping *Mockingbird*, a group of nine black teenagers, aged thirteen to nineteen, were accused of raping two white women on board a train in Alabama. The Scottsboro Boys, as they came to be

Research: The introduction informs you that the Scottsboro Boys were repeatedly tried and retried. Research the history of this case. Find out what happened to each of the nine young men involved in the case.

known, were repeatedly tried, retried, and sentenced to death for the assault, despite a lack of physical evidence and the fact that one of the supposed victims recanted. The two excerpts below, written by Clarence Norris (with Sybil Washington) and Haywood Patterson (with Earl Conrad), two of the Scottsboro boys, describe attempts to lynch the young men, first when they were removed from the train and second, shortly after, as they awaited trail in a jail in Scottsboro, Alabama.

The Last of the Scottsboro Boys: An Autobiography
By Clarence Norris and Sybil D. Washington

[The excerpt begins with a description of how the train Norris has been riding stops in Paint Rock, Alabama, and he finds himself facing a mob.]

When I looked up, the tracks were lined with a *mob* of men. They had sticks, pistols, rifles, shotguns; everything you need to murder, they had it. . . . We were surrounded by a sea of white faces, screaming, "Let's hang these black sons of bitches. Where's the rope for these niggers?"

Two men had on uniforms. I don't know if they were police, firemen or soldiers, but they saved our lives. . . . The men in the uniform said, "Let's take them to jail." . . . We were taken to the nearest jail, in Scottsboro, Alabama. That's why we are called the Scottsboro Boys today.

. . .

Next day we were taken from the cage and put in a line. The sheriff brought two women over to us. He said, "Miss Price, which one of these niggers had you?" She went down the line pointing her finger: "This one, this one, this one . . ." until she picked out six, including me. . . . I blurted out that it was a lie. Before I could blink that guard struck out at me with his *bayonet*. I threw up my hands and he slashed my right hand open to the bone. He screamed, "Nigger, you know damn well how to talk about white women."

They shoved us back into the cage. I was scared before, but it wasn't nothing to how I felt now. I knew if a white woman accused a black man of rape, he was as good as dead. . . . All I could think was that

Reflect on the title: The excerpt is subtitled "An Autobiography" but lists both Clarence Norris and Sybil D. Washington as coauthors. Why might Norris have chosen to write his autobiography with another person? What difference might that make to your evaluation of his words and ideas?

Notice the image here: "We were surrounded by a sea of white faces." How does this figurative language complicate the earlier description of the tracks as "lined with a mob of men"? What tone is set by this language?

Notice that the initial threat of violence is thwarted by two men in uniform. Why do you think Norris is unable to identify who these two men are? Are you surprised to hear Norris write that being taken to jail was a lifesaver?

Reflect: What do you think of how the sheriff proceeds? Do the boys seem to be treated as if they are innocent or guilty? Do you think the witness identification of the attackers seems to have been handled carefully?

Vocabulary: The sheriff asks Price to identify which of the men "had" her. What does he mean? Why do you think the sheriff might have used a euphemism here?

I was going to die for something I had not done. I had never seen those two women before in my life.

Norris, Clarence and Sybil D. Washington. *The Last of the Scottsboro Boys: An Autobiography*. New York: Putnam, 1979: 19–22. Print.

[The next excerpt takes up the story shortly after this accusation is made, as the young men wait in the jail.]

Scottsboro Boy
By Haywood Patterson and Earl Conrad

Round about *dusk* hundreds of people gathered about the jail-house. "Let the niggers out," they yelled. We could hear it coming in the window. "If you don't, we're coming in after them." White folks were running around like mad ants, white ants, sore that somebody had stepped on their hill. We heard them yelling like crazy how they were coming in after us and what ought to be done with us. "Give 'em to us," they kept screaming, till some of the guys, they cried like they were seven or eight years old. . . .

Reflect: How do the guard's actions and word choices reflect attitudes of the time?

Key idea: Norris articulates how dangerous it was for a black man to be accused of raping a white woman. Why do you think this accusation, within a jail cell, makes Norris feel more scared than he was before, facing a mob of white men?

Reflect on the title: Notice that this autobiography is also coauthored and that Patterson, like Norris, takes for his title a variation on the term, "Scottsboro boy." What do you think about that?

Notice the language used here: "White folks were running around like mad ants, white ants, sore that somebody had stepped on their hill." What is the effect of comparing the mob here to mad, white ants? What do you think of Patterson's remark that it was as if the ants were "sore that somebody stepped on their hill"?

As evening came on the crowd got to be to about five hundred, most of them with guns. Mothers had kids in their arms. Autos, bicycles, and wagons were parked around the place. People in and about them.

Two or three deputies, they came into our cell and said, "All right, let's go." They wanted to take us out to the crowd. They handcuffed us each separately. Locked both our hands together. Wanted to rush us outside into the hands of that mob. We fellows hung close, didn't want for them to put those *irons* on. You could see the look in those deputies' faces, already taking some funny kind of *credit* for turning us over.

Patterson, Haywood and Earl Conrad. *Scottsboro Boy*. Garden City, NY: Doubleday, 1950: 7–8. Print.

> **Notice** that Patterson describes mothers with "kids in their arms." Why do you think he includes this detail? What effect does it have on you as a reader?
>
> **Key idea:** Unlike the earlier excerpt, Patterson describes two or three public officials who don't intend to save the boys' lives. What do the deputies intend here? How does this scene reflect Norris's earlier fear that a black man accused of raping a white woman "was as good as dead"?

CHECK FOR UNDERSTANDING   RI.9-10.1, RI.9-10.4, RI.9-10.6

1. Norris writes: "Before I could blink that guard struck out at me with his bayonet." In other words,
   a) he struck the guard in the blink of an eye.
   b) the guard struck him immediately.
   c) the guard struck him in the eye.
   d) the guard struck him without looking.

2. When Norris writes that he was "surrounded by a sea of white faces," he is implying that
   a) all white people look alike.
   b) he felt under water.
   c) he was in a dangerous position.
   d) he was attacked by the white people.

3. When the sheriff asked Miss Price to identify her assailants, he asked her "which one of these niggers had you?" In this sentence, he is using
   a) a racist epithet
   b) a euphemism
   c) both a and b
   d) neither a nor b

4. Patterson's main goal in describing the deputies' actions is
   a) to show how racist white people are.
   b) to show how powerful the mob is.
   c) to show how even the police collaborated with lynch mobs.
   d) to show how the police could be lifesavers.

5. When Patterson describes how some of the boys were crying "like they were seven or eight years old," his purpose is to emphasize
   a) how terrifying the situation was.
   b) how young the Scottsboro Boys were.
   c) how childish the Scottsboro Boys were.
   d) how badly the boys felt about the crime they had committed.

WRITING AND DISCUSSION

RI.9-10.1, RI.9-10.2, RI.9-10.3, RI.9-10.4, RI.9-10.5, RI.9-10.6, W.9-10.2, W.9-10.4, W.9-10.5, W.9-10.9, SL.9-10.1, L.9-10.1, L.9-10.2, L.9-10.3, L.9-10.5

A. How did it feel to be a Scottsboro Boy?

1. **Discuss:** In the two excerpts you have read, the two Scottsboro Boys tell us something about how they felt at the moment they were taken off the train and then put into jail. What emotions do they describe?

2. **Discuss:** Both Norris and Patterson use figurative language to describe the white mobs they face. Norris calls the mob a "sea of white faces" and Patterson calls the white people a gang of "mad ants, white ants." Analyze their language choices here. In these two examples, how do Norris and Patterson see the white mobs? How are their language choices similar? How are they different?

3. **Discuss:** Both Norris and Patterson use a variety of specific details to paint a picture of the mobs they face. What specific details strike you? How do they use these details to gain sympathy for themselves and indict the behavior of most of the white people around them, except the two uniformed men who save the boys by taking them to jail? *Use Table A-1 to organize a list of details about the white people Norris and Patterson face.*

4. **Write:** How do Norris and Patterson use figurative language, details, and emotional language to show their readers how terrifying it felt to be a Scottsboro Boy? *Use evidence from both excerpts in your response.*

Table A-1: Details about White People

Text	Textual evidence	Your interpretation	Effect on reader
Norris	"They had sticks, pistols, rifles, shotguns; everything you need to murder, they had it."	The mob of white men was armed to the teeth.	The unarmed, teenage Norris is in a position of tremendous vulnerability against this armed group of men.

B. What was a lynch mob like?

RL.9-10.1, RL.9-10.2, RL.9-10.4, RL.9-10.5,
RI.9-10.1, RI.9-10.2, RI.9-10.5, W.9-10.1, W.9-
10.4, W.9-10.5, W.9-10.9, SL.9-10.1, L.9-10.1,
L.9-10.2, L.9-10.3, L.9-10.5

1. **Discuss:** In the introduction and the two excerpts you have read, you have learned something about the characteristics of lynching in the United States. *Use the first two columns of Table B-1 to list some of these characteristics.*

2. **Discuss:** Search the lynching scene in chapter 15 of *Mockingbird*. Which characteristics of lynching do you find there? Which characteristics are absent? *Use the third and fourth columns of Table B-1 to compare the lynching scene in* Mockingbird *to your earlier observations about the characteristics of lynching.*

3. **Write:** Compare Harper Lee's depiction of the lynch mob that comes to execute Tom Robinson with the lynch mobs faced by Clarence Norris and Haywood Patterson. What do you think about the differences? Which do you find more threatening? *Use evidence from* Mockingbird *and the Norris and Patterson excerpts in your response.*

Table B-1: Characteristics of a Lynch Mob

Characteristics of lynching	Textual evidence	Comparison with Mockingbird	Textual evidence
Police are actively involved in allowing the mob to exact its extrajudicial justice.	The deputies "Wanted to rush us outside into the hands of that mob."	Sheriff Tate's men don't actively aid the lynch mob. Are they somewhat complicit in allowing themselves to fall for the "snipe hunt" ruse and be lured away?	"Heck's bunch's so deep in the woods they won't get out till mornin'."
	`		

C. Is the Klan really gone, Atticus?

RL.9-10.1, RL.9-10.2, RL.9-10.3, RI.9-10.1, RI.9-10.2, W.9-10.1, W.9-10.4, W.9-10.5, W.9-10.7, W.9-10.8, W.9-10.9, SL.9-10.1, L.9-10.1, L.9-10.2, L.9-10.3, L.9-10.5

1. **Discuss:** In chapter 15, Atticus and Jem have a conversation about the Ku Klux Klan (KKK). What does Atticus tell Jem? Are you surprised by Atticus's opinion of and attitude toward the Klan? What is the significance of Atticus's comments about Sam Levy, clearly a Jewish target of the Klan?

2. **Research:** Research the nature of the KKK in the 1920s and 1930s. Whom did the Klan target? What kinds of activities did they carry out? In what ways does Atticus's description of the Klan match the information you uncover in your research?

3. **Discuss:** In the first half of chapter 15, a crowd of men, including Sheriff Tate, gathers at Atticus's house. Scout says grown men only stand outside to talk for two reasons: "death and politics." What concerns do the men raise? How does Atticus respond to their concerns? *Use Table C-3 to chart the issues.*

4. **Write:** Use the experiences of Clarence Norris and Haywood Patterson and your research about the Klan to reflect on Atticus's attitudes and behavior in chapter 15. Is Atticus brave or foolish? Do you think he underestimates the danger to Tom Robinson in Maycomb? *Use evidence from* Mockingbird, *the Norris and Patterson excerpts, and your research in your response.*

Table C-1: Death and Politics

Concerns of the men	Textual evidence	Atticus's response	Textual evidence	Interpretation
Sheriff Tate says that Tom Robinson will be moved to the county jail tomorrow and hints that he is worried about his safety.	"I don't look for any trouble, but I can't guarantee there won't be any."	Atticus doesn't think there will be trouble.	"Don't be foolish, Heck. . . . This is Maycomb."	Perhaps Atticus underestimates the danger to Tom Robinson and the nature of Maycomb.

CLASS ACTIVITY

RL.9-10.1, RL.9-10.3, RI.9-10.1, RI.9-10.2, RI.9-10.3, RI.9-10.4, RI.9-10.5, RI. 9-10.6, W.9-10.1, W.9-10.2, W.9-10.3, W.9-10.4, W.9-10.5, W.9-10.6, W.9-10.7, W.9-10.8, W.9-10.9, SL.9-10.1, SL.9-10.2, SL.9-10.4, SL.9-10.5, SL.9-10.6, L.9-10.1, L.9-10.2, L.9-10.3, L.9-10.5, L.9-10.6

Task: Your goal is to produce two of the following three news reports by Mr. Underwood for the *Maycomb Tribune*. Remember that Scout tells us that "Mr. Underwood had no use for any organization but the *Maycomb Tribune*, of which he was the sole owner, editor, and printer." Remember as well that Mr. Underwood lives above the Maycomb jail and witnesses the entire attempted lynching of Tom Robinson.

1. **Research news coverage of the Scottsboro Boys.** How was the case covered by national media? Research and read through the online coverage of the case available on the *New York Times* website.
2. **Write two of the following three news reports:**
   a. **Write a news report by Mr. Underwood about the Scottsboro Boys.** Think carefully about how this independent, Maycomb newsman would have seen and reported the case. What details and facts would he have included? How would he have anticipated and/or attempted to shape public opinion? What relevance, do you think, would this case have had for Maycomb and how would that have shaped Underwood's coverage? How would his coverage of the case differ from what you see in the *New York Times*?
   b. **Write a news report by Mr. Underwood about the attempted lynching of Tom Robinson.** Would he have represented this incident in a two-line news report or would he have devoted significant time and space to the event? What details and facts would he have included? How would he have anticipated and/or attempted to shape public opinion?
   c. **Write Mr. Underwood's editorial about the killing of Tom Robinson in prison.** Scout references this editorial at the end of chapter 25, but we don't actually get to read it as part of the novel. Review what Scout says about the editorial, including the fact that Mr. Underwood "was at his most bitter" and "likened Tom's death to the senseless slaughter of songbirds by hunters and children."
3. **Other visuals.** Mr. Underwood would likely include some pertinent and suggestive pictures that illustrate the issues in these stories. You have a wide variety of visuals from the time period available to you online and/or at your school or local library. Which would Mr. Underwood use, if any? Think, in particular, about whether he would have taken and used photos in his report about the Maycomb incident and whether he would or would not identify anyone by name.

4. **You will present your news report in class.** During your presentation, you will explain the components of your project, what choices you made, and what you were trying to accomplish. Be prepared to answer questions about your work.

In addition, each individual must produce:

5. **A narrative explanation.** Write a narrative in which you explain what your group was trying to accomplish and the choices you made in fulfilling the requirements of the assignment (the length of the news reports, the details in the news reports, the particular pictures included). Justify (with textual evidence) why you think Underwood would have covered the events as you suggest. In particular, discuss how and why you think Underwood's coverage would differ from what you found in the *New York Times*.
6. **A discussion of your group dynamic.** Write a narrative in which you explain your role in the group. What tasks did you take responsibility for? How successfully did you collaborate with your peers? What struggles did your group face in tackling the project?

CLASS ACTIVITY RUBRIC

Category	4—Excellent	3—Good	2—Satisfactory	1—Unsatisfactory
News articles	Articles show outstanding understanding of and insight into the texts, issues, and characters	Articles show good understanding of and insight into the texts, issues, and characters	Articles show limited or uneven understanding of and insight into the texts, issues, and characters	Articles show insufficient or inaccurate understanding of and insight into the texts, issues, and characters
Visuals (strategic use of media in presentations; integration of diverse media)	Project makes effective use of strategic visuals	Project makes good use of strategic visuals	Project makes limited or uneven use of strategic visuals	Project makes insufficient or ineffective use of strategic visuals
Narrative explanation (cite relevant and sufficient textual evidence)	Narrative explanation is clear, coherent, and shows excellent insight into the texts and issues	Narrative explanation is solid and shows good insight into the texts and issues	Narrative explanation is limited or uneven and shows some insight into the texts and issues	Narrative explanation is unclear and/or incoherent and shows little insight into the texts and issues
Collaboration (initiate and participate effectively in collaboration)	Student takes responsibility for his or her own work; collaborates well with others; negotiates group dynamics well	Student takes responsibility for his or her own work; collaborates sufficiently with others; shows some success negotiating group dynamics	Student takes limited responsibility for his or her own work; collaborates minimally with others; attempts to negotiate group dynamics	Student takes no responsibility for his or her own work; student does not collaborate with others; student struggles to or is unable to negotiate group dynamics
Vocabulary (use domain-specific vocabulary)	Several "words to own" from the unit are used correctly	Some "words to own" from the unit are used correctly in articles and/or narratives	One or more "words to own" from the unit are used but perhaps not correctly or effectively in articles and/or narratives	No "words to own" from the unit are used in articles and/or narratives
Class presentation (presentation of knowledge and ideas)	Presentation of the project is effective, concise, logical, and organized	Presentation of the project is generally but not fully effective, concise, logical, and organized	Presentation of the project is somewhat effective, but with some issues of brevity, logic, and organization	Presentation of the project is not effective, with serious problems in brevity, logic, and organization

UNIT 6

What's Up with Mr. Dolphus Raymond?

Chief Justice Earl Warren, Loving v. Virginia

TEACHER'S GUIDE
Overview

Harper Lee introduces an irreverent character, Mr. Dolphus Raymond, who provides an intriguing counterstory to the drama of Mayella Ewell and Tom Robinson. In chapter 16, the children hear of Raymond and his "colored woman and all sorts of mixed chillun." In chapter 20, the children speak with Raymond and learn that he only pretends to be drunk in order to temper the judgment of white society. Students need to understand the specifics of the taboo and law Raymond was breaking by engaging in an interracial relationship. A brief reading from the 1967 Supreme Court case, *Loving v. Virginia*, allows students to see that in the 1930s, when the novel was set, and even in 1960, when the novel was published, interracial marriage was still considered criminal behavior in some areas of the United States. Reading *Loving v. Virginia* allows students to appreciate the historical context for Dolphus Raymond's behavior and to reflect on this important case in our nation's history.

Timing

This brief reading can be used just prior to or just after students read chapters 16 and 20 (the critical chapters involving Dolphus Raymond).

Consider the following guidelines regarding when to undertake the different activities:

Essential question for discussion and writing	Objective	Suggested timing	Suggested rubric	Additional research
A. Why not marry the one you love?	Students will (SW) research antimiscegenation laws in order to write an essay exploring whether a white man in Alabama (or elsewhere) could marry the woman he loves.	any time—although this set of questions mentions Dolphus Raymond, it doesn't require any knowledge of the character and could be used to set up the issues in chapters 16 and 20	B	Y
B. What's the real story behind Dolphus Raymond?	SW explore the "fraud" of Dolphus Raymond in order to understand his behavior in the context of antimiscegenation laws and prevailing attitudes toward interracial relationships.	after chapter 20 (when the children begin to uncover Dolphus Raymond's "fraud")	A	N

Notes on the Article

- The reading contains a substantial amount of difficult vocabulary, some difficult syntax, and some potentially unfamiliar content references (nativism, miscegenation, etc.), so teachers should be sure to take their time with both the vocabulary warm-up and the reading questions/prompts.
- Some sections of the decision have been omitted, including discussion of the appeals process leading up to *Loving v. Virginia* and substantial and complex legal discussion of earlier and related opinions and court decisions.
- Key vocabulary: repugnant, miscegenation, statute, appellant, scheme, incident, nativism, patently, legitimate, invidious, repudiated, odious, subversive

Suggested Media Links

- *The Loving Story* (HBO, 2012)
- Song: Nancy Griffith's "The Loving Kind" (2009)
- "Remembering Mr. and Mrs. Loving" interview with the Lovings' attorney, Bernard Cohen, available on YouTube
- Loving Day: a website established in 2004 and devoted to multicultural awareness and education about tolerance and the history of interracial relationships

VOCABULARY WARM-UP

L.9-10.4, L.9-10.5, L.9-10.6

Words to own: repugnant, miscegenation, statute, appellant, scheme, incident, nativism, patently, legitimate, invidious, repudiated, odious, subversive

Section A: Use context clues. Read the following sentences and use context clues to determine the meaning of the italicized words.

1. The Lovings argued that Virginia's statutes against marriages between blacks and whites were *repugnant* to the Fourteenth Amendment. What do you think it means for the statutes to be *repugnant* to the Fourteenth Amendment? Explain.

2. The word "*miscegenation*" was coined in a propaganda pamphlet in 1863 to refer to and raise alarm about intermarriage between blacks and whites. *Miscegenation* is derived from the Latin *miscere*, "to mix," and *genus*, "kind." Do you think those who coined this term believed intermarriage between blacks and whites to be a good or bad thing? What does the etymology of the word tell you about how they thought about the difference between black and white people?

3. In overturning the lower court decisions and ruling against the constitutionality of the statutes under consideration, Justice Warren writes that the racial classifications in those statutes are "*subversive* of the principle of equality at the heart of the Fourteenth Amendment." Based on the context here, does this mean the racial classifications support the principle of equality or undermine that principle?

4. Justice Warren explains that Virginia's "Racial Integrity Act of 1924, passed during the period of extreme *nativism* which followed the end of the First World War." *Nativists* in the 1920s were concerned with the racial purity of the United States and worried that immigrants and others were diluting what they saw as the American racial stock. Based on this context, do you think the Racial Integrity Act would support or prohibit interracial marriage? What would *nativists* think of interracial marriage?

Section B: More context clues. Here your task is to use context clues to understand the word's meaning and to practice your context clues skills.

1. Though some *statutes* may remain part of a state's legal system, some truly outdated *statutes* are no longer enforced. *Statutes* here means
    a) laws
    b) judges
    c) court cases
    d) branches

2. Which word from the sentence in question 1 best helps the reader to understand the meaning of *statutes*?
    a) remain
    b) system
    c) legal
    d) outdated

3. I find the rule completely *odious*; as a person of character and integrity, I will do my best to overturn the hateful rule. *Odious* here means
    a) offensive
    b) smelly
    c) malodorous
    d) horrified

4. Which word from the sentence in question 3 best helps the reader to understand the meaning of *odious*?
    a) character
    b) person
    c) rule
    d) hateful

Section C: Use the dictionary in order to understand the uncommon meanings of these common words.

1. When Warren writes that "There is *patently* no legitimate overriding purpose" for the statutes' use of racial classification, he isn't talking about a patent as an exclusive right, as in a patent on an invention. He uses the word *patently* in order to make what point about the purpose of the statutes?

2. "Penalties for miscegenation arose as an *incident* to slavery and have been common in Virginia since the colonial period." What does Warren mean by as an *incident* to slavery? In your own words, explain the relationship between slavery and penalties for miscegenation.

3. The Supreme Court ruled: "Virginia's statutory *scheme* to prevent marriages between persons solely on the basis of racial classifications held to violate the Equal Protection and Due Process Clauses of the Fourteenth Amendment." Is the Supreme Court suggesting that the state of Virginia is secretly trying to keep people of different races from marrying each other?

Section D: Use the dictionary to look up the italicized words and answer the following questions based on their definitions.

1. If I am an *appellant* in a case, can you tell whether I am innocent or guilty?

2. The court found there to be no *legitimate* purpose for racial classification in this case. If the racial classification wasn't used for legitimate purposes, why was it used?

3. The politician's remarks to the crowd were *invidious*. As a result, how might the young people in the crowd have responded to the politician's speech? What recommendation would you make to the politician about his next public event?

4. Politicians are often asked to *repudiate* comments made by supporters. For example, President Obama was asked to *repudiate* comments made by Reverend Jeremiah Wright. Would you be willing to *repudiate* a close friend if she said something you didn't agree with? Why or why not?

5. The politician may have intended to be *subversive* in his remarks against marriage equality, but her loud and regular public commentary about the evils of same-sex marriage ended up drawing attention, and eventually support, to gay and lesbian rights. What does this result suggest about the politician's strategy? In this case, how might she have been more effectively *subversive*?

6. Some people feel that the SATs are part of a devious *scheme* designed to ensure the misery of all high school students. What other elements of high school might be a part of this grand and evil *scheme* to inflict misery on teenagers?

Section E: Practice using the word correctly by choosing the right form of the word that best fits in the blank within the following sentences.

1. I ask you to _____ your earlier comments; they suggest a racist attitude that is incompatible with student leadership.
   a) repudiated
   b) repudiate
   c) repudiates
   d) repudiation

2. In hindsight, we can see that the Racial Integrity Act of 1924 was a _____ racist law.
   a) patent
   b) patents
   c) patently
   d) patented

3. From what we know, the Lovings were not intending to be _____ when they married; they were simply two people in love who wanted to be together. They weren't trying to change laws or rewrite history.
   a) subvert
   b) subversive
   c) subverts
   d) subversion

4. The Lovings were the _____ in this case; the state of Virginia was the other party in the case.
   a) appellants
   b) appeal
   c) appealing
   d) appealed

Section F: Vocabulary skits. Use the model sentences and definitions to understand the words in question. Create a skit in which you address the given topic. Every member of the group must use the vocabulary word at least once during your performance of the skit.

1. *invidious*—hateful, offensive, causing ill will or resentment
   ▪ It was a small miracle that no fight broke out after her *invidious* remarks at the meeting.

- Jim Crow Laws were a series of *invidious* practices designed to keep black people from achieving economic or social equality.
- The U.S. military is struggling against a pattern of *invidious* sexual harassment and sexual assault against women in the military.

Scenario: A middle school is facing a pattern of *invidious* behavior involving bullying. Create a skit in which several high school students serve as panelists at a middle school assembly on bullying. The high school students' task is to help their younger peers understand how *invidious* bullying can be.

2. *odious*—hateful, offensive, disgusting
   - Some people find the smell of a high school cafeteria to be *odious*; others find the smell merely distasteful; few find the smell attractive.
   - Some complain that our current airport security screenings are *odious* and unnecessary in a free and open society; others insist that the conditions of our world today necessitate that we make peace with unpleasant and uncomfortable practices.
   - Some researchers argue that not only is homework an *odious* and detestable chore, but that it serves little good in furthering students' learning.

Scenario: Create a skit in which a group of students, as a punishment for their tardiness, is given the *odious* task of cleaning the school's bathrooms. As they clean the bathrooms, they complain about how *odious* they find the task while also bemoaning the injustice of the punishment they face.

3. *nativism*—the practice of protecting the interests of native inhabitants against immigrants, usually considered to be an ethnocentric and/or racist ideology
   - Virginia's Racial Integrity Act of 1924 was passed during a period of *nativism* following World War I.
   - *Nativism* is usually associated with an attempt to protect people and ideas from a perceived outside threat.
   - Is it racist *nativism* or healthy nationalism if a country tries to close its borders to all immigrants wishing to move to the country?

Scenario: Create a skit in which a group of politicians discusses a solution to the problem of illegal immigration in the United States. As the debate grows heated, several politicians are accused of trying to disguise *nativist* ideas as honest public policy.

ESSENTIAL QUESTION:
WHAT'S UP WITH MR.
DOLPHUS RAYMOND?
Introduction

Loving v. Virginia (1967) was a landmark civil rights decision. The case involved a black woman, Mildred Loving, and a white man, Richard Loving, who travelled in June 1958 to the District of Columbia in order to marry. One night, after they returned to Virginia to live together as husband and wife, police raided their home based on an anonymous tip and charged them with violating Virginia's ban on interracial marriage, Virginia's Racial Integrity Act of 1924. Mildred Loving protested to Attorney General Robert F. J. Kennedy, who referred her to the American Civil Liberties Union (ACLU). The ACLU took up the case, and a series of lawsuits ensued, ending with the final suit in the United States Supreme Court. Chief Justice Earl Warren wrote the unanimous decision of the court, overturning the Virginia law and lower court decisions. Although unenforceable after the *Loving* decision, many state interracial marriage bans remained on the books long after. In 2000, after a ballot initiative, Alabama became the last state in the United States to remove the prohibition on interracial marriage.

> **Reflect on the essential question:** What does the question suggest to you?
>
> **Reflect on the introduction:** The introduction tells you that the piece you are about to read was written by the Chief Justice of the United States Supreme Court about a court case in 1967. Where does that case stand in historical relation to the setting of *Mockingbird*? Which came first, the publication of *Mockingbird* or *Loving v. Virginia*?
>
> **Key idea:** What does it mean that Chief Justice Warren "wrote the unanimous opinion of the court"? Did all the other court justices agree with Justice Warren? Is that always the case? What happens if someone disagrees with the justice who writes the majority opinion?

Loving v. Virginia
APPEAL FROM THE SUPREME COURT OF APPEALS OF VIRGINIA. No. 395.

Argued April 10, 1967.

Decided June 12, 1967.

Virginia's *statutory scheme* to prevent marriages between persons solely on the basis of racial classifications held to violate the Equal Protection and Due Process Clauses of the Fourteenth Amendment.

    . . .

MR. CHIEF JUSTICE WARREN delivered the opinion of the Court.

This case presents a constitutional question never addressed by this Court: whether a *statutory scheme* adopted by the State of Virginia to prevent marriages between persons solely on the basis of racial classifications violates the Equal Protection and Due Process Clauses of the Fourteenth Amendment. For reasons which seem to us to reflect the central meaning of those constitutional commands, we conclude that these *statutes* cannot stand consistently with the Fourteenth Amendment.

In June 1958, two residents of Virginia, Mildred Jeter, a Negro woman, and Richard Loving, a white man, were married in the District of Columbia pursuant to its laws. Shortly after their marriage, the Lovings returned to Virginia and established their marital abode in Caroline County. At the October Term, 1958, of the Circuit Court of Caroline County, a grand jury issued an indictment charging the Lovings with violating Virginia's ban on interracial marriages. On January 6, 1959, the Lovings pleaded guilty to the charge and were sentenced to one year in jail; however, the trial judge suspended the sentence for a period of 25 years on the condition that the Lovings leave the State and not return to Virginia together for 25 years. He stated in an opinion that:

Reflect on the title of the case: Who does the Loving in *Loving v. Virginia* stand for? What does the v. stand for? Who is Virginia? Why was the case argued in April but not decided until June?

Key idea: Section 1 of the Fourteenth Amendment states that: "All persons born or naturalized in the United States, and subject to the jurisdiction thereof, are citizens of the United States and of the State wherein they reside. No State shall make or enforce any law which shall abridge the privileges or immunities of citizens of the United States; nor shall any State deprive any person of life, liberty, or property, without *due process* of law; nor deny to any person within its jurisdiction the *equal protection* of the laws."
     Put this amendment into your own words. What do you think due process is? What do you think equal protection means? What does it mean that states cannot deprive a person of equal protection without due process?

Key idea: Justice Warren focuses on the Fourteenth Amendment in relation to the Virginia statutes. When he concludes the statutes cannot stand consistently with the Fourteenth Amendment, what does he mean?

Reflect: Why do you think Jeter and Loving left Virginia to get married? Why do you think they might have returned home to Virginia instead of staying in the District of Columbia where their marriage was legal? Why do you think they pleaded guilty to the charges against them?

Almighty God created the races white, black, yellow, malay and red, and he placed them on separate continents. And but for the interference with his arrangement there would be no cause for such marriages. The fact that he separated the races shows that he did not intend for the races to mix.

> **Notice** that the trial judge suggests that the races should not mix because God placed them on separate continents. Why do you think he makes the rhetorical choice to invoke "Almighty God" here? What purpose does this serve for his argument?
>
> **Reflect:** After their conviction, the Lovings took up residence in the District of Columbia where their marriage was legal. Why do you think they decided to continue with their legal appeals?

After their convictions, the Lovings took up residence in the District of Columbia. On November 6, 1963, they filed a motion in the state trial court to . . . set aside the sentence on the ground that the statutes which they had violated were *repugnant* to the Fourteenth Amendment. The motion not having been decided by October 28, 1964, the Lovings instituted a class action in the United States District Court for the Eastern District of Virginia requesting that a three-judge court be convened to declare the Virginia *anti-miscegenation statutes* unconstitutional.

. . .

The two *statutes* under which *appellants* were convicted and sentenced are part of a comprehensive *statutory scheme* aimed at prohibiting and punishing interracial marriages. The Lovings were convicted of violating 20-58 of the Virginia Code:

> *Leaving State to evade law. If any white person and colored person shall go out of this State, for the purpose of being married, and with the intention of returning, and be married out of it, and afterwards return to and reside in it, cohabiting as man and wife, they shall be punished as provided in 20-59, and the marriage shall be governed by the same law as if it had been solemnized in this State.* The fact of their cohabitation here as man and wife shall be evidence of their marriage.

Section 20-59, which defines the penalty for *miscegenation*, provides:

> *Punishment for marriage. If any white person intermarry with a colored person, or any colored person intermarry with a white person, he shall be guilty of a felony and shall be punished by confinement in the penitentiary for not less than one nor more than five years.*

Other central provisions in the Virginia *statutory scheme* are 20-57, which automatically voids all marriages between "a white person and a colored person" without

---

any judicial proceeding, and 20-54 and 1-14 which, respectively, define "white persons" and "colored persons and Indians" for purposes of the statutory prohibitions. The Lovings have never disputed in the course of this litigation that Mrs. Loving is a "colored person" or that Mr. Loving is a "white person" within the meanings given those terms by the Virginia statutes.

Virginia is now one of 16 States which prohibit and punish marriages on the basis of racial classifications. Penalties for miscegenation arose as an *incident* to slavery and have been common in Virginia since the colonial period. The present *statutory scheme* dates from the adoption of the Racial Integrity Act of 1924, passed during the period of extreme *nativism* which followed the end of the First World War. The central features of this Act, and current Virginia law,

Note: A footnote in the decision explains that the Virginia law only prohibits "whites" from marrying non-"whites": "While Virginia prohibits whites from marrying any nonwhite (subject to the exception for the descendants of Pocahontas), Negroes, Orientals, and any other racial class may intermarry without statutory interference. Appellants contend that this distinction renders Virginia's miscegenation statutes arbitrary and unreasonable even assuming the constitutional validity of an official purpose to preserve 'racial integrity.'" What do you think about this element of the Virginia law?

Notice that Justice Warren uses quotation marks around the "white person" and "colored person" and writes about "meanings" for these terms given by the Virginia statutes. Why do you think he does this? What do you think of these terms? Do you understand why they would need to be defined by statute?

Vocabulary: Justice Warren writes that antimiscegenation laws "arose as an incident to slavery." What does he mean? What connection is there between antimiscegenation laws and slavery?

are the absolute prohibition of a "white person" marrying other than another "white person," a prohibition against issuing marriage licenses until the issuing official is satisfied that the applicants' statements as to their race are correct, certificates of "racial composition" to be kept by both local and state registrars, and the carrying forward of earlier prohibitions against racial intermarriage.

. . .

There can be no question but that Virginia's *miscegenation statutes* rest solely upon distinctions drawn according to race. The statutes proscribe generally accepted conduct if engaged in by members of different races. Over the years, this Court has consistently

Key idea: Justice Warren associates the antimiscegenation statutes with "the period of extreme *nativism* which followed the end of the First World War." In this way, he places the statutes within a larger historical and cultural context. How does understanding the statutes in this context make a difference?

repudiated "[d]istinctions between citizens solely because of
their ancestry" as being *odious* to
a free people whose institutions
are founded upon the doctrine of
equality." *Hirabayashi v. United
States*, 320 U.S. 81, 100 (1943). At
the very least, the Equal Protection
Clause demands that racial classifications, especially suspect in criminal statutes, be subjected to the
"most rigid scrutiny," *Korematsu
v. United States*, 323 U.S. 214, 216
(1944), and, if they are ever to be
upheld, they must be shown to be

> **Key idea:** Warren quotes an earlier court decision here that distinctions based on ancestry have been repudiated as odious to a free people. Put this idea into your own words.
>
> **Key idea:** Warren writes that two members of the court (two of the justices) have stated that the color of a person's skin cannot be the test of whether a person's conduct is criminal. How would Virginia's statutes banning interracial marriage make the color of a person's skin a test of whether his conduct is a criminal offense? Explain.

necessary to the accomplishment of some permissible state objective, independent of
the racial discrimination which it was the object of the Fourteenth Amendment to
eliminate. Indeed, two members of this Court have already stated that they "cannot
conceive of a valid legislative purpose . . . which makes the color of a person's skin the
test of whether his conduct is a criminal offense." *McLaughlin v. Florida*, supra, at 198
(STEWART, J., joined by DOUGLAS, J., concurring).

There is *patently* no *legitimate* overriding purpose independent of *invidious* racial
discrimination which justifies this classification. The fact that Virginia prohibits only
interracial marriages involving white persons demonstrates that the racial classifications must stand on their own justification, as measures designed to maintain White
Supremacy. We have consistently denied the constitutionality of measures which re-
strict the rights of citizens on account of race. There can be no doubt that restricting
the freedom to marry solely because of racial classifications violates the central meaning of the Equal Protection Clause.

II.

These statutes also deprive the Lovings of liberty without due process of law in violation of the Due Process Clause of the Fourteenth Amendment. The freedom to marry
has long been recognized as one of the vital personal rights essential to the orderly
pursuit of happiness by free men.

Marriage is one of the "basic civil rights of man," fundamental to our very existence
and survival. *Skinner v. Oklahoma*, 316 U.S. 535, 541 (1942). . . . To deny this fundamental freedom on so unsupportable a basis as the racial classifications embodied in
these statutes, classifications so directly *subversive* of the principle of equality at the

heart of the Fourteenth Amendment, is surely to deprive all the State's citizens of liberty without due process of law. The Fourteenth Amendment requires that the freedom of choice to marry not be restricted by *invidious* racial discriminations. Under our Constitution, the freedom to marry, or not marry, a person of another race resides with the individual and cannot be infringed by the State.

Key idea: What is White Supremacy? What connection is Warren suggesting here between the ban on interracial marriage and White Supremacy?

Discuss: Warren argues here that marriage is a basic civil right. What does that mean to you? Why would supporters of marriage equality want to use *Loving v. Virginia* to build a case for same-sex marriage?

These convictions must be reversed.

It is so ordered.

Loving v. Virginia. Supreme Court. 12 June 1967. Print.

CHECK FOR UNDERSTANDING   RI.9-10.1, RI.9-10.4, RI.9-10.6, RI.10.9

1. Warren writes: "The two statutes under which appellants were convicted and sentenced are part of a comprehensive statutory scheme aimed at prohibiting and punishing interracial marriages." He means here:
   a) The statutes were part of a plot to punish black people.
   b) The Lovings were found guilty under two statutes designed to prevent interracial marriage.
   c) The Lovings are appealing an unjust scheme against interracial marriage.
   d) The statutes are an unfair prohibition against interracial marriage.

2. Which of the following is NOT true about the case in question?
   a) The Lovings were married in the District of Columbia.
   b) Virginia's marriage laws were unrelated to slavery.
   c) The Lovings left the state of Virgina after being convicted of violating Virginia law.
   d) Virginia law prohibited all interracial marriages.

3. Warren's main goal in writing this piece is to
   a) explain his ideas about the Virginia law.
   b) explain the court's decision in this case.
   c) explain his decision in this case.
   d) explain why the Lovings should have been allowed to marry.

4. Warren writes that "There is patently no legitimate overriding purpose independent of invidious racial discrimination which justifies this classification." This sentence suggests that
   a) Warren accepts racial discrimination as legitimate.
   b) Warren doesn't understand the purpose of racial discrimination.
   c) Racial discrimination justifies the classification of certain marriages as criminal.
   d) Warren finds no legitimate purpose other than racism for classifying certain marriages as criminal.

5. Warren quotes another court decision, *Skinner v. Oklahoma*: "marriage is one of the 'basic civil rights of man,' *fundamental* to our very existence and survival." By *fundamental*, Warren means
   a) basic
   b) civil
   c) right
   d) existential

WRITING AND DISCUSSION

RI.9-10.1, RI.9-10.9, W.9-10.2 W.9-10.4,
W.9-10.5, W.9-10.7, W.9-10.8, W.9-10.9,
SL.9-10.1, L.9-10.1, L.9-10.2, L.9-10.3

A. Why not marry the one you love?

1. **Research and Discuss:** Writing in 1967, Justice Warren indicates that Virginia is one of sixteen states that "prohibit and punish marriages on the basis of racial classifications." Conduct some basic research on how interracial marriage was handled historically in Alabama and in your state.

   - What were the laws involving marriage between a black person and a white person in Alabama in 1930?

   - Were interracial marriage laws ever passed in your state? Did they apply to all races or only marriages involving whites?

   - If your state had antimiscegenation laws, were these laws repealed before *Loving v. Virginia*?

2. **Write:** Chapter 16 features a white man, Dolphus Raymond, who "lives by himself way down near the county line. He's got a colored woman and all sorts of mixed chillun." Could he marry the woman he loves? Use your understanding of the laws against interracial marriage to discuss the options for a white man like Raymond who wanted to live with a colored woman in Alabama in 1930. Include a discussion of what marital options existed for a white man living in your state in 1930. *Use evidence from your research and from Loving in your response.*

B. What's the real story behind Dolphus Raymond?

RL.9-10.1, RL.9-10.2, RL.9-10.3, RL.9-10.4, RI.9-10.1, RI.9-10.2, RI.9-10.3, RI.9-10.9, W.9-10.2 W.9-10.4, W.9-10.5, W.9-10.9, SL.9-10.1, L.9-10.1, L.9-10.2, L.9-10.3, L.9-10.5

1. **Discuss:** Use *Loving v. Virginia* to discuss attitudes toward interracial relationships. What does Loving tell you about attitudes toward those relationships in 1967? What do you think attitudes toward interracial relationships would have been like in a place like Maycomb, Alabama, in the 1930s?

2. **Discuss:** In chapter 16, the children encounter a series of rumors or misconceptions about Dolphus Raymond. For example, Jem thinks Raymond drinks whiskey all day long from a Coca-Cola bottle. Some of these misconceptions are cleared up in chapter 20; Dill discovers that the drink in the sack is "Just plain Coca-Cola." *Use Table B-1 to list what the children think they know about Raymond and what they discover about Raymond.*

3. **Discuss:** Some aspects of the character of Dolphus Raymond are relatively straightforward. The children think one thing about Raymond, but they find out they are wrong. Other questions about Raymond, however, are never fully or clearly resolved. *Given what you know about antimiscegenation laws and racism, use Table B-2 to try to offer some explanation for some of the unresolved questions about Raymond.*

4. **Write:** What's the real story behind Dolphus Raymond? Consider how laws against interracial marriage and the attitudes toward interracial relationships that those laws reflect serve to produce Raymond as "a being who deliberately perpetrated fraud against himself." In answering this question, discuss both the understanding the children come to have of Raymond's "fraud" as well as your own conjectures about Raymond's real story. *Use evidence from* Mockingbird *and from* Loving *in your response.*

Table B-1: Dolphus Raymond: Rumor versus Reality

Rumor or misconceptions	Textual evidence	Clarification	Textual evidence
Raymond is a drunk.	"He's got a Co[ca]-Cola bottle full of whiskey in there. . . . You'll see him sip it all afternoon."	Raymond only pretends to drink whiskey; the bottle is full of Coca-Cola.	"'You mean all you drink in that sack's Coca-Cola?' . . . 'Yes ma'am,' Mr. Raymond nodded."

Table B-2: Dolphus Raymond: Unresolved Questions

Unresolved question	Textual evidence	Possible explanation or interpretation
Does Raymond sits with black people because he likes them better than white people?	"He likes 'em better'n he likes us, I reckon."	Raymond may not be allowed to sit with white people. Because of his taboo relationship, he may be generally unwelcome in white society.

Is Atticus a Hero?

David Margolick, "To Attack a Lawyer in To Kill a Mockingbird: *An Iconoclast Takes Aim at a Hero"*

TEACHER'S GUIDE
Overview

David Margolick's "To Attack a Lawyer in *To Kill a Mockingbird*: An Iconoclast Takes Aim at a Hero," originally published in the *New York Times*, summarizes a dispute between legal scholars about whether Atticus Finch should be considered a hero or even an exemplary lawyer. Discussion of this article will give students the opportunity to analyze these arguments based on their understanding of the novel, evaluate Atticus and his words and actions in the context of the novel, and also consider whether it's appropriate to judge someone from the past—whether a real-life or fictional character—based on our cultural or social standards today.

Timing

This article is best used after students have read at least through chapter 23 or have finished the book.

Consider the following guidelines regarding when to undertake the different activities:

Discussion and writing	Objective	Suggested timing	Suggested rubric	Additional research
A. How does Margolick open his case in order to win the interest and attention of his readers?	Students will (SW) analyze Margolick's use of allusion and rhetorical questions in order to write an essay evaluating how he wins the interest and attention of his readers.	any time—this set of questions doesn't require any knowledge of *Mockingbird*	B	Y
B. Is Atticus a hero?	SW analyze the ideas of Monroe Freedman and Timothy Hall in order to determine whether Atticus should be considered a hero.	after students have completed the novel or after chapter 9 (when Atticus explains how he came to represent Tom Robinson)	B	Y
C. Is Atticus racist?	SW analyze the ideas of Monroe Freedman in order to consider whether Atticus is racist or complicit in the racism of the events of the novel.	after students have completed the novel or after chapter 24 (when Atticus and everyone learn of the death of Tom Robinson)	A	N
D. Is Atticus sexist?	SW analyze Atticus and Aunt Alexandra's treatment of Scout in order to consider whether Atticus is sexist.	after chapter 9 (Scout's visit to Finch's Landing) or after chapter 13 (when Aunt Alexandra comes to live with Scout and her family)	A	N
E. How do we judge the behavior of people from the past?	SW analyze the issue of present-day standards of behavior versus contemporary standards of behavior in order to consider whether it is fair to judge Atticus by today's standards.	after students have completed the novel but could be used in a limited way after chapter 23 (Atticus and Jem's discussion of the trial)	A	N

Discussion and writing	Objective	Suggested timing	Suggested rubric	Additional research
Class Activity				
School board hearing	SW enact and analyze a school board hearing on whether *Mockingbird* should be taught, centered around the question: "Is Atticus a hero?"	after chapter 9 (Scout's altercation with Cecil Jacobs) or any time later	Rubric included	Y

Notes on the Article

- Students may have trouble with the fairly dated reference to psychic Jeanne Dixon at the beginning of the article, but it offers an opportunity for students to identify and analyze an allusion and its impact and to discuss why the author chose to begin the article that way. This aspect of the article is addressed in one of the "Check for Understanding" questions.

- While this article offers students the opportunity to evaluate opposing arguments based on their knowledge of the novel, it is important that they understand that this is a newspaper article discussing the two points of view and that the writer of the article isn't advocating either side. This point is addressed in one of the "Check for Understanding" questions and an extended writing prompt.

- The reading contains a substantial amount of difficult vocabulary, so teachers should take their time with the vocabulary warm-up and the reading questions/ prompts.

- Key vocabulary: iconoclast, heterodox, prognostications, avuncular, duck, sagacious, clairvoyant, countenance, unsullied, emulate, noblesse oblige, contrariness, sacred cow, reclusive, nefarious, zealously, bigoted, exemplar

Suggested Media Links

- Online video clips about segregation in the South during the 1930s can supplement students' background knowledge about the realities of the period.

- PBS.org hosts a set of multimedia resources called "The Rise and Fall of Jim Crow," which includes an interactive timeline, audio and video recordings of people who lived through segregation, and links to rare documents. The site features resources on key events, organizations (including the NAACP [National Association for the Advancement of Colored People]), and individuals associated with the history of the Jim Crow laws.

- Online video clips about the history of the NAACP can help students understand what Atticus working for the organization, as Freedman suggests, would have meant.

VOCABULARY WARM-UP

L.9-10.4, L.9-10.5, L.9-10.6

> **Words to own:** iconoclast, heterodox, prognostications, avuncular, duck, sagacious, clairvoyant, countenance, unsullied, emulate, noblesse oblige, contrariness, sacred cow, reclusive, nefarious, zealously, bigoted, exemplar

Section A: Use context clues. Read the following sentences and use context clues to determine the meaning of the italicized words.

1. "In her *prognostications* for 1992, the psychic Jeanne Dixon predicted that 'anti-lawyer riots will shake the profession.'" Based on the context, what do you think a *prognostication* is? What is Dixon's *prognostication* here?

2. "But could even the canniest *clairvoyant* have foreseen an attack on Atticus Finch?" Based on the context in which it is used, what do you think a *clairvoyant* is?

3. "Later, to spare the reclusive Boo Radley from a murder prosecution, [Atticus] *countenances* Sheriff Heck Tate's fiction that the nefarious Bob Ewell actually fell upon his own knife." Based on the context, what does it mean to *countenance* something? What does Atticus *countenance*?

4. Jones discusses whether Finch represents Tom Robinson due to "an elitist sense of *noblesse oblige*." If an elitist is someone who considers himself superior in intellect, power, or social position and "*noblesse oblige*" means, in French, the obligation of the nobility, what would it mean for Finch to represent Tom Robinson out of a sense of "*noblesse oblige*"?

Section B: More context clues. Here your task is to use context clues to understand the word's meaning and to practice your context clues skills.

1. Archie Bunker was a television character well known for his *bigoted*, racist comments about people different from himself. *Bigoted* here means
   a) different
   b) well known
   c) prejudiced
   d) open-minded

2. Which word from the sentence in question 1 helps the reader understand the meaning of *bigoted*?

   a) racist

   b) television

   c) character

   d) people

3. Freedman argues that Atticus has been seen as an "ethical *exemplar*" and that lawyers may see him as someone to emulate or model themselves after. *Exemplar* here means

   a) problem

   b) lawyer

   c) example

   d) argument

4. Which word from the sentence in question 3 helps the reader understand the meaning of *exemplar*?

   a) ethical

   b) lawyer

   c) argues

   d) model

Section C: Use the dictionary in order to understand the uncommon meanings of the following common words.

1. Introducing legal scholar Monroe Freedman, Margolick writes that Freedman "has never been one to *duck* controversy." What does it mean to *duck* controversy? Can you see any connection between this meaning of the word and the animal by the same name known for swimming in ponds?

2. Margolick explains that "In telling his children to pity their grumpy, bigoted neighbor, Mrs. Henry Lafayette Dubose, because she was addicted to morphine, [Atticus] was arguably betraying a client's confidence." What does he mean by *confidence*? What does it mean to betray someone's *confidence*? How does Atticus betray Mrs. Dubose's confidence?

Section D: Use the dictionary to look up the italicized words and answer the following questions based on their definitions.

1. Whom do you consider to be *avuncular* and why?

2. Would you expect an *iconoclast* to display *contrariness*? Why?

3. Would you most want to *emulate* someone who is *sagacious*? Why?

4. Would a *sacred cow* be considered *heterodox*? Why or why not?

5. Would you rather be considered *nefarious* or *reclusive*? Why?

6. If you were in legal trouble, would you want your lawyer to defend you *zealously*? Why?

7. Children sometimes have difficulty keeping their clothes *unsullied*. Why?

Section E: Practice using the word correctly by choosing the correct form of the word that best fits in the blank within the following sentences.

1. _____ someone who does foolish things is not a wise decision.
   a) Emulation
   b) Emulating
   c) Emulate
   d) Emulates

2. Because the election polls showed that the presidential race was very close, no one could confidently _____ its outcome.
   a) prognosis
   b) prognostication
   c) prognosticate
   d) prognosticating

3. The twins were always _____ with each other; if one said "yes," the other would say "no."
   a) contrariness
   b) contrarily
   c) contrary
   d) contrarian

4. I don't understand why the principal _____ the cafeteria food; I wish he would stop tolerating the mediocre slop and insist that we receive higher quality, more nutritious school lunches.
   a) countenanced
   b) countenances
   c) countenance
   d) would countenanced

5. I want to keep my school record clean and _____ so that I will be attractive to colleges and future employers; therefore, I always do my best to stay out of trouble.
   a) unsully
   b) unsullies
   c) sullied
   d) unsullied

Section F: Vocabulary skits. Use the model sentences and definitions to understand the words in question. Create a skit in which you address the given topic. Every member of the group must use the vocabulary word at least once during your performance of the skit.

1. *iconoclast*—a person who attacks or criticizes cherished or established beliefs, ideas, institutions, or values
   - Many consider Lady Gaga an *iconoclast* for the ways in which she has refused to conform to expectations in her image and music.
   - I saw my refusal to attend religious services as an expression of my radical ideas; my parents, however, refused to accept me as an *iconoclast*.
   - Some historians think that the women burned as witches in Salem were really *iconoclasts* who challenged their society's beliefs and paid with their lives.

     Scenario: Create a skit in which several high school students address the board of education in protest over the district school uniform policy. The students maintain that they are *iconoclasts* and that the uniform policy does not allow them to express their opposition to the traditional dress code.

2. *contrariness*—being oppositional, willful, or stubborn, the state of being contrary
   - Teenagers sometimes value *contrariness* in and of itself; they strive to avoid conformity at all costs.
   - My mother sometimes accuses me of being *contrary*, but I feel I have a right to assert myself and my ideas.

- If you dismiss my opposition to the new law as *contrariness*, you risk underestimating the serious concerns that I, and others, have to the new law.

  Scenario: Create a skit in which the president of the United States is meeting with several lawmakers from different parties to discuss his proposal to address climate change. They raise a number of objections to his proposal, and he insists they are being *contrary*.

3. *clairvoyant*—claiming to be psychic, be able to have visions, be prophetic
   - My father claimed to be *clairvoyant*, but it didn't take any special powers to tell that the cloudy sky was about to open up into a downpour of rain.
   - If I were *clairvoyant*, I think I would use my special powers to predict the lottery results and win lots and lots of money.
   - Perhaps it would be quite miserable to be *clairvoyant*; I'm not sure I would be happy knowing the future each and every day of my life.

   Scenario: Create a skit in which several young people decide to go see a psychic. As she tells their futures, each of them reacts differently, some accepting the vision, others challenging whether or not she really is *clairvoyant*.

4. *sagacious*—wise, shrewd, smart
   - My grandfather was the most *sagacious* person I've ever known; he was truly a wise old man.
   - It is difficult for the young to be *sagacious*; they are full of ideas and energy but short on experience.
   - Getting good grades in school is no guarantee of *sagacity*; a person may know all the answers to the test questions and still lack real wisdom and intelligence.

   Scenario: Create a skit in which a young man and his friends are discussing how upset they are about the outcome of a recent court case in the national news. The kids reflect on how to voice their protest effectively. One student shares her experiences with social protest. As she speaks, her *sagacity* inspires her friends to listen carefully to her ideas and consider what specific actions to pursue.

ESSENTIAL QUESTION:
IS ATTICUS A HERO?
Introduction

Since the publication of *To Kill a Mockingbird*, Atticus Finch has stood as a symbol of moral courage and the ideal lawyer, not only in English classes but in law school ethics courses as well. According to this *New York Times* article by David Margolick, at least one prominent legal scholar disagrees with that opinion.

Reflect on the essential question: What does the question suggest to you? How might Atticus be defined as a hero? Why might someone not consider him a hero?

Reflect on the introduction: The introduction tells you that the piece you are about to read is a newspaper article about a legal scholar's criticisms of Atticus. What criticisms do you think he might have? Given that newspaper articles are supposed to be objective, what else would you expect Margolick to include in his article?

To Attack a Lawyer in *To Kill a Mockingbird*: An Iconoclast Takes Aim at a Hero
By David Margolick

In her *prognostications* for 1992, the psychic Jeanne Dixon predicted that "anti-lawyer riots will shake the profession." But could even the canniest *clairvoyant* have foreseen an attack on Atticus Finch?

Atticus Finch, the *sagacious* and *avuncular* lawyer-hero of Harper Lee's 1960 novel, "To Kill a Mockingbird," who earned the scorn of his segregated Southern town by defending a black man wrongly accused of rape? Atticus Finch, who stood down a lynch mob that had

Reflect on the title: "To Attack a Lawyer in *To Kill a Mockingbird*: An Iconoclast Takes Aim at a Hero." Why does the writer construct the title in this way? What does the title tell us about the legal scholar who is criticizing Atticus?

Notice how Margolick begins his article. Why does he make reference to Jeanne Dixon? What point is he trying to make? What does it mean to be the "canniest clairvoyant"?

Notice how the second paragraph continues with several rhetorical questions about Atticus? What is the purpose of these questions? What impact do they have on the reader?

come to collect his client one night at the Maycomb jail? Atticus Finch, who taught a community and his two young children about justice, decency and tolerance, and who drove a generation of real-life Jems and Scouts to become lawyers themselves?

Monroe Freedman of Hofstra Law School has never been one to *duck* controversy. His *heterodox* views on what constitutes vigorous representation of a client once led Chief Justice Warren E. Burger to call for his disbarment. Now, in his column on professional ethics, which appears monthly in "Legal Times," Mr. Freedman has taken on Atticus Finch.

Legal scholars concede that Finch has his ethical lapses. In telling his children to pity their grumpy, *bigoted* neighbor, Mrs. Henry Lafayette Dubose, because she was addicted to morphine, he was arguably betraying a client's confidence. Later, to spare the *reclusive* Boo Radley from a murder prosecution, he *countenances* Sheriff Heck Tate's fiction that the *nefarious* Bob Ewell actually fell upon his own knife.

But in legal literature as much as in the popular imagination, Finch, particularly Gregory Peck's film version of the man, has heretofore remained *unsullied*. In his trailblazing 1981 law review article, "The Moral Theology of Atticus Finch," Thomas Shaffer of Notre Dame Law School described Finch as someone "who risks everything in order to tell the truth." Two years ago, Timothy Hall of the University of Mississippi Law School wrote of Finch, "Truthfulness was stamped upon his character like an Indian head on an old nickel."

All this is too much for the *iconoclastic* Mr. Freedman. "Atticus Finch has become the ethical *exemplar* in articles on topics ranging from military justice to moral theology," he writes. "If we don't do something fast, lawyers are going to take him seriously as someone to *emulate*. And that would be a bad mistake."

Sure, Mr. Freedman writes, Finch represented Tom Robinson *zealously*, and for nothing in return. But he took the case involuntarily—failure to accept the court-ordered appointment could have landed him in what Miss Lee called Maycomb's "miniature Gothic joke" of a jail for contempt—and only

Vocabulary: Margolick writes that Freedman's "heterodox views on what constitutes vigorous representation of a client once led Chief Justice Warren E. Burger to call for [Freedman's] disbarment." What is he saying? What does "disbarment" mean? Put this into your own words.

Key idea: Margolick lists two "ethical lapses" committed by Atticus. What is an "ethical lapse"? Do these lapses make Atticus a bad lawyer?

Vocabulary: According to Margolick, "in legal literature as much as in the popular imagination, Finch . . . has heretofore remained unsullied." What does it mean for a person to be "unsullied"? Put this in your own words.

Notice that Margolick lists several examples here. What purpose do these examples serve? What does Timothy Hall's figurative statement, "truthfulness was stamped on [Atticus's] character like an Indian on an old nickel," mean?

Key idea: According to Margolick, "All this is too much for the *iconoclastic* Mr. Freedman." What is "too much" for Freedman? What makes Freedman "iconoclastic"? What does this mean?

"from an elitist sense of *noblesse oblige.*" Besides, Mr. Freedman asked, what had Finch done up to that point to combat the forces that brought Robinson down?

Far from attacking racism at its root, Mr. Freedman charges, Finch was *complicit* in it. For all his gentlemanliness, he does not complain that blacks attending court are relegated to the balcony. He eats in segregated restaurants; he walks in parks where signs say "No Dogs or Colored Allowed." And he is too willing to excuse racism in others, dismissing the local chapter of the Ku Klux Klan as "a political organization more than anything else," and the leader of the lynch mob as "basically a good man" with "blind spots."

> **Key idea:** Margolick summarizes some of Freedman's criticisms of Atticus. According to Freedman, why is Atticus's defense of Tom Robinson not necessarily so admirable? What does he mean by "an elitist sense of *noblesse oblige*"?
>
> **Key idea:** Margolick paraphrases Freedman's argument here that Atticus was "complicit" in racism. What does Freedman mean by that? Why is he arguing that Atticus is complicit in racism?

More than a racist, Finch is a sexist. Mr. Freedman notes that in his closing argument to the jury Finch dismisses Eleanor Roosevelt as "the distaff side of the executive branch in Washington." Worse, while encouraging Jem to follow in his footsteps and become a lawyer, he does not similarly encourage his daughter. "Scout understands that she will be some gentleman's lady," Mr. Freedman writes.

Professors Shaffer and Hall, both of whom regularly assign "To Kill a Mockingbird" in their legal ethics classes, good-naturedly accuse Mr. Freedman of *compulsive contrariness.* "There isn't a *sacred cow* in the world Monroe Freedman doesn't enjoy taking on," Mr. Shaffer said. In addition, they accused Mr. Freedman of what Mr. Hall called "chronological snobbery"; that is, unfairly subjecting a New Deal–era Alabama lawyer to contemporary standards of behavior.

> **Key idea:** Why do Shaffer and Hall accuse Freedman of "*compulsive contrariness*"? How does Freedman's enjoyment of taking on "*scared cow[s]*" connect with what they see as his "*compulsive contrariness*"?
>
> **Key idea:** Hall here compares Atticus to a prophet and parish priest. What is the purpose of this rhetorical move here? What point is Hall making about Atticus?

Mr. Freedman, they added, also has a mistaken notion of perfection, one that would require lawyers not only to stand vigilantly by their oppressed clients, but also to separate themselves entirely from all agents of oppression.

"What Monroe really wants is for Atticus to be working on the front lines for the N.A.A.C.P. in the 1930's, and if he's not, he's disqualified from being any kind of hero," Mr. Hall said. "Monroe has this vision of lawyer as prophet. Atticus has a vision of lawyer not only as prophet, but as parish priest."

Margolick, David. "To Attack a Lawyer in To Kill a Mockingbird: An Iconoclast Takes Aim at a Hero." *Nytimes.com.* The New York Times, 28 Feb. 1992. Web. 3 Feb. 2014.

CHECK FOR UNDERSTANDING

RI.9-10.1, RI.9-10.4, RI.9-10.5, RI.9-10.6

1. According to the article, Freedman's *"heterodox* views on what constitutes vigorous representation of a client once led Chief Justice Warren E. Burger to call for his disbarment." By *heterodox*, the writer means
   a) unethical
   b) nontraditional
   c) inexperienced
   d) irrational

2. The article quotes Freedman as saying, "If we don't do something fast, lawyers are going to take him seriously as someone to emulate." What is Freedman's concern?
   a) Lawyers won't live up to Atticus's example.
   b) Lawyers will consider Atticus an expert on military justice.
   c) Lawyers will follow Atticus as an example.
   d) Lawyers will stop representing unpopular clients.

3. In the article, law professor Thomas Shaffer criticizes Freedman by saying, "There isn't *a sacred cow* in the world Monroe Freedman doesn't enjoy taking on." By *sacred cow*, Shaffer means
   a) a cow that is worshipped as a god
   b) a difficult legal case
   c) a widely and strongly held belief
   d) a controversial subject

4. Which of the following details does NOT support Freedman's argument that Atticus is not a hero or a good lawyer?
   a) Atticus did not protest against segregated parks and restaurants.
   b) Atticus did not encourage Scout to be a lawyer.
   c) Atticus stood up against a lynch mob who was coming after his client.
   d) Atticus told his children about Mrs. Dubose's morphine addiction.

5. Margolick's main goal in writing this article seems to be
   a) to defend Atticus Finch as an honorable hero.
   b) to argue that Atticus Finch doesn't deserve so much respect.
   c) to inspire more people to read *To Kill a Mockingbird*.
   d) to summarize opposing viewpoints held by legal scholars about Atticus.

WRITING AND DISCUSSION

RI.9-10.1, RI.9-10.4, RI.9-10.5, RI.9-10.6, W.9-10.1,
W.9-10.2, W.9-10.4, W.9-10.5, W.9-10.7, W.9-10.9,
SL.9-10.1, L.9-10.1, L.9-10.2, L.9-10.3, L.9-10.6

A. **How does Margolick open his case in order to win the interest and attention of his readers?**

1. **Research and discuss:** The first sentence of the article contains an allusion, that is, a reference, in this instance, to the clairvoyant Jeanne Dixon.

   > In her *prognostications* for 1992, the psychic Jeanne Dixon predicted that "anti-lawyer riots will shake the profession." But could even the canniest clairvoyant have foreseen an attack on Atticus Finch?

   Who is Jeanne Dixon? What do you think of the use of this allusion as the opening for this article?

2. **Discuss:** What do you notice about the sentence structure in the second paragraph?

   > Atticus Finch, the *sagacious* and *avuncular* lawyer-hero of Harper Lee's 1960 novel, "To Kill a Mockingbird," who earned the scorn of his segregated Southern town by defending a black man wrongly accused of rape? Atticus Finch, who stood down a lynch mob that had come to collect his client one night at the Maycomb jail? Atticus Finch, who taught a community and his two young children about justice, decency and tolerance, and who drove a generation of real-life Jems and Scouts to become lawyers themselves?

   What purpose do you think is served by Margolick's rhetorical choice here?

3. **Write:** Consider Margolick's choices in beginning his article this way and analyze and evaluate what impact they have on the reader. How does Margolick open his case in order to win the interest and attention of his readers? *Use evidence from Margolick in your response.*

B. Is Atticus a hero?

RL.9-10.1, RL.9-10.3, RI.9-10.1, RI.9-10.2, W.9-10.1, W.9-10.2, W.9-10.4, W.9-10.5, W.9-10.7, W.9-10.8, W.9-10.9, SL.9-10.1, L.9-10.1, L.9-10.2

1. **Discuss:** Freedman notes that while Atticus defended Tom Robinson to the best of his ability, he did not take the case voluntarily. He had been appointed to represent Robinson and would have ended up in jail himself if he had refused.
   - Is this true? What exactly does Atticus say about how he came to represent Robinson, and how does he feel about it? Find evidence from the text on this point.
   - In your opinion, how does this affect whether Atticus should be considered a hero or not?

2. **Research and discuss:** The article ends with a quote from law professor Timothy Hall: "What Monroe [Freedman] really wants is for Atticus to be working on the front lines for the N.A.A.C.P. in the 1930's, and if he's not, he's disqualified from being any kind of hero," Mr. Hall said.
   - What is the NAACP? What does it do?
   - What would it have meant for Atticus to have worked for the NAACP in the 1930s?

3. **Write:** Should Atticus be considered a hero? Why or why not? *Use evidence from Margolick, your research about the NAACP, and Mockingbird in your response.*

C. Is Atticus racist?

RL.9-10.1, RL.9-10.2, RL.9-10.3, RI.9-10.1, RI.9-10.2, W.9-10.1, W.9-10.4, W.9-10.5, W.9-10.9, SL.9-10.1, L.9-10.1, L.9-10.2

1. **Discuss:** What does it mean to be complicit with racism? If someone doesn't object to racism at every opportunity, does it mean he or she is a racist?

2. **Discuss:** Freedman argues that, while Atticus does vigorously defend Tom Robinson, he doesn't do much about the racism in his society that put Robinson in the position of being falsely accused and convicted.

> Far from attacking racism at its root, Mr. Freedman charges, Finch was complicit in it. For all his gentlemanliness, he does not complain that blacks attending court are relegated to the balcony. He eats in segregated restaurants; he walks in parks where signs say "No Dogs or Colored Allowed." And he is too willing to excuse racism in others, dismissing the local chapter of the Ku Klux Klan as "a political organization more than anything else," and the leader of the lynch mob as "basically a good man" with "blind spots."

Consider this criticism in relation to the actions of other characters in the novel. *Use Table C-1 to compare the characters in terms of how racist or not racist you think each is.*

3. **Write:** Is Atticus racist? Is Atticus complicit with the racism of Maycomb county? Pick three examples in which Atticus and other characters in the novel talk about or do something in relation to the treatment of African American men and women. If they are not "attacking racism at its root," are they still racist or complicit in the persistence of racism? *Use evidence from Margolick and* Mockingbird *in your response.*

Table C-1: Complicit with Racism?

Character	Actions in relation to race/racism	Textual evidence	Your judgment
Judge Taylor	Judge Taylor appoints Atticus to defend Tom Robinson instead of an inexperienced lawyer, but he doesn't set aside Robinson's conviction by the jury. Judge Taylor also doesn't do anything about the black citizens of Maycomb being forced to sit in the balcony of his own courtroom.	"Court-appointed defenses were usually given to Maxwell Green, Maycomb's latest addition to the bar, who needed the experience. Maxwell Green should have had Tom Robinson's case." "The Colored balcony ran along three walls of the courtroom like a second-story veranda"	Judge Taylor is willing to challenge the injustice of racism indirectly and behind the scenes; he is unwilling to take any personal and/or public stand against racism.

D. Is Atticus sexist?

RL.9-10.1, RL.9-10.2, RL.9-10.3, RI.9-10.1, W.9-10.1, W.9-10.4, W.9-10.5, W.9-10.9, SL.9-10.1, L.9-10.1, L.9-10.2

1. **Discuss:** What does "sexism" mean? Where and how is "sexism" present in to-day's society?

2. **Discuss:** According to the article, Freedman charges Atticus with sexism because "while encouraging Jem to follow in his footsteps and become a lawyer, he does not similarly encourage his daughter." Do you agree with Freedman? Do you think Atticus treats Scout differently than Jem? Consider Atticus's treatment of his daughter in chapters 9, 10 and 14. What qualities/characteristics does Atticus seem to care about developing in Scout? *Use Table D-1 to organize examples that highlight Atticus's expectations for Scout.*

3. **Discuss:** Consider Aunt Alexandra's attempts to make Scout into a lady in chapters 9, 13, 14, and 24. How does she go about that? What qualities/characteristics does Aunt Alexandra seem to care about developing in Scout? *Use Table D-2 to highlight the different ways in which Aunt Alexandra expresses her expectations for Scout.*

4. **Write:** Pick three examples of sexism in the novel and use them to consider two or more of the following questions: Is Atticus sexist? Does Atticus treat Scout differently than Jem because she is a girl? Does Atticus support Scout's independence? *Use evidence from Margolick and* Mockingbird *in your response.*

Table D-1: Atticus's Attitude toward Scout

Aspects of Atticus's attitude toward Scout	Evidence	Interpretation
Atticus continues to read to Scout, even when Miss Caroline says he shouldn't.	"If you'll concede the necessity of going to school, we'll go on reading every night just as we always have."	Atticus thinks it's important that Scout is educated and informed, despite the expectations others, like Miss Caroline, might have for her.

Table D-2: Aunt Alexandra Makes Scout into a Lady

Aunt Alexandra's attitude towards Scout	Evidence	Interpretation
Cares about Scout's unladylike dress.	"Aunt Alexandra was fanatical on the subject of my attire. I could not possibly hope to be a lady if I wore breeches."	A woman's appearance is important.

**E. How do we judge the behavior
of people from the past?**

RL.9-10.1, RL.9-10.3, RI.9-10.1, RI.9-10.2, RI.9-
10.3, RI.9-10.5, RI.9-10.6, RI.9-10.8, W.9-10.1,
W.9-10.4, W.9-10.5, W.9-10.7, W.9-10.8, W.9-
10.9, SL.9-10.1, L.9-10.1, L.9-10.2, L.9-10.3

1. **Discuss:** Is it appropriate to judge people in the past according to our standards and beliefs today? Why or why not?

2. **Research:** Research and discuss practices and customs from the past that we might find inappropriate or wrong today: gender-segregated want ads (Help Wanted Men, Help Wanted Women); race-segregated schools; women not being allowed to vote.

3. **Discuss:** According to the article, law professors Shaffer and Hall "accused Mr. Freedman of what Mr. Hall called 'chronological snobbery'; that is, unfairly subjecting a New Deal–era Alabama lawyer to contemporary standards of behavior." Using the article, identify moments when Freedman might be holding Atticus accountable to present-day standards of behavior rather than the standards of behavior of Atticus's own 1930s society. *Use Table E-1 to catalog and analyze examples of what Shaffer and Hall call "chronological snobbery."* Do you think it is fair of Freedman to hold Atticus accountable to present-day standards?

4. **Write:** Do you think it is fair to judge Atticus according to today's standards? Why or why not? Should we judge people's attitudes and actions in the past based on the beliefs we hold today? *Use evidence from Margolick, your research on practices and customs from the past, and* Mockingbird *in your response.*

Table E-1: "Chronological Snobbery"

Example of "chronological snobbery" in Freedman	Textual evidence of this "chronological snobbery"	Your assessment of this "chronological snobbery"
Freedman condemns Atticus for excusing racism.	Atticus is "too willing to excuse racism in others, dismissing the local chapter of the Ku Klux Klan as 'a political organization more than anything else.'"	Perhaps in 1930, some white Americans would have thought of the KKK as a political organization; today it is considered a hate group.

A L A

CLASS ACTIVITY

RL.9-10.1, RL.9-10.2, RL.9-10.3, RI.9-10.1, RI.9-10.2, RI.9-10.3, RI.9-10.4, RI.9-10.5, RI. 9-10.6, RI.9-10.8, W.9-10.1, W.9-10.3, W.9-10.4, W.9-10.5, W.9-10.9, SL.9-10.1, SL.9-10.3, SL.9-10.4, SL.9-10.6, L.9-10.1, L.9-10.2, L.9-10.3, L.9-10.6

Task: Your goal is to conduct a school board hearing debating the question of whether *To Kill a Mockingbird* should be part of the school curriculum. For the purposes of the debate, the school board is considering whether or not the text offers, in Atticus, an appropriate hero for children to emulate. The debate, therefore, focuses on the following question: "Is Atticus a hero?"

Parts:
    school board members
    parents
    teachers
    the school principal
    expert witnesses (journalist David Margolick, law professor Monroe Freedman, law
        professor Thomas Shaffer, law professor Timothy Hall)

In addition, each student must produce the following:

1. **Explanation of your role:** Write a narrative in which you explain how you went about determining how you would play your part and what you decided to say during the hearing. Justify (with textual evidence) how your contributions during the hearing were informed by your understanding of *Mockingbird* and of Margolick's text.
2. **Posthearing evaluation:** (1) Write a narrative in which you evaluate how the school board hearing was conducted. Discuss how well your classmates played their parts: Did their words and actions make sense for their roles? (2) Reflecting on Margolick's editorial, *Mockingbird*, as well as the exchange of ideas during the hearing, discuss the essential question: "Is Atticus a hero?" Has your position changed in any way? Why or why not?

CLASS ACTIVITY RUBRIC

Category	4—Excellent	3—Good	2—Satisfactory	1—Unsatisfactory
Performance of role (presentation of knowledge and ideas)	Performance demonstrates strong and insightful comprehension of role through ample, effective reference to evidence from Margolick and novel	Performance demonstrates solid comprehension of role through frequent, effective reference to evidence from Margolick and novel	Performance demonstrates some comprehension of role through occasional, though perhaps vague or ineffective, reference to evidence from Margolick and novel	Performance does not demonstrate comprehension of role through reference to evidence from Margolick and novel
Collaboration (initiate and participate effectively in conversation and collaboration)	Student participates clearly and persuasively in debate	Student participates somewhat clearly and persuasively in debate	Student participates somewhat clearly but perhaps not persuasively in debate	Student does not participate clearly or persuasively in debate
Explanation of role (cite relevant and sufficient textual evidence)	Narrative demonstrates strong and insightful comprehension of role through ample, effective reference to evidence from Margolick and novel	Narrative demonstrates solid comprehension of role through frequent, effective reference to evidence from Margolick and novel	Narrative demonstrates some comprehension of role through occasional, though perhaps vague or ineffective, reference to evidence from Margolick and novel	Narrative does not demonstrate comprehension of role through reference to evidence from Margolick and novel
Hearing evaluation and reflection (cite relevant and sufficient textual evidence)	Evaluation and reflection make clear, insightful arguments based on substantial specific evidence from debate and texts	Evaluation and reflection make clear arguments based on specific evidence from debate and texts	Evaluation and reflection make arguments that may be vague or not clearly based on evidence from debate and texts	Evaluation and reflection do not make arguments based on evidence from debate and texts
Vocabulary (use domain-specific vocabulary)	Several "words to own" from the unit are used correctly in debate and/or narratives	Some "words to own" from the unit are used correctly in debate and/or narratives	One or more "words to own" from the unit are used but perhaps not correctly or effectively	No "words to own" from the unit are used in debate and/or narratives
Documentation (in-text citation and works cited)	Essay(s) conform to the appropriate style guidelines (MLA) for in-text citation and works cited	Essay(s) conform with limited errors to the appropriate style guidelines (MLA) for in-text citation and works cited	Essay(s) attempt to conform to the appropriate style guidelines (MLA) for in-text citation and works cited but do so ineffectively or inaccurately	Essay(s) do not conform to the appropriate style guidelines (MLA) for in-text citation and works cited

Rubrics

RUBRIC A

Category	4—Excellent	3—Good	2—Satisfactory	1—Unsatisfactory
Examples (cites relevant and sufficient textual evidence)	Essay uses and discusses thoroughly a wide range of examples	Essay uses and discusses a wide range of examples although the discussion of these examples may be incomplete or uneven	Essay uses and discusses some examples although the discussion of these examples may be incomplete or uneven	Essay uses and discusses a limited number of examples and discusses these minimally
Focused and cohesive argument (valid reasoning and organization)	Essay makes a focused and cohesive argument in response to prompt	Essay makes an argument in response to prompt, but the argument may not be fully cohesive or focused throughout	Essay makes an uneven and not particularly clear argument in response to prompt	Essay makes no real argument in response to prompt
Insight and understanding (determines the meaning of and analyzes text)	Essay shows significant insight into and understanding of the text	Essay shows some insight into and understanding of the text	Essay shows limited insight into and understanding of the text	Essay shows little insight into and understanding of the text
Grammar and mechanics (conventions of standard English)	Essay contains few errors in grammar and mechanics, and they do not inhibit meaning; no patterns of error	Essay contains some errors in grammar and mechanics, and they do not inhibit meaning; errors do not fall into patterns	Essay contains frequent errors in grammar and mechanics that may inhibit meaning; writing exhibits some patterns of error	Essay contains numerous errors in grammar and mechanics that inhibit meaning; writing exhibits several patterns of error
Vocabulary use (uses domain-specific vocabulary)	Essay uses precise, varied, and strong vocabulary; several "words to own" from the unit are used correctly	Essay uses some precise, varied, and strong vocabulary; essay attempts to use "words to own" from the unit, but these may be used infrequently or with limited accuracy	Vocabulary choices are sometimes imprecise, repetitive, and weak; essay does not attempt to use "words to own" from the unit or uses these ineffectively and inaccurately	Vocabulary choices are vague, repetitive, and weak; essay does not attempt to use "words to own" from the unit
Documentation (in-text citation and works cited)	Essay conforms to the appropriate style guidelines (MLA) for in-text citation and works cited	Essay conforms with limited errors to the appropriate style guidelines (MLA) for in-text citation and works cited	Essay attempts to conform to the appropriate style guidelines (MLA) for in-text citation and works cited but does so ineffectively or inaccurately	Essay does not conform to the appropriate style guidelines (MLA) for in-text citation and works cited

RUBRIC B

Category	4—Excellent	3—Good	2—Satisfactory	1—Unsatisfactory
Examples (cites relevant and sufficient textual evidence)	Essay uses and discusses thoroughly a wide range of examples	Essay uses and discusses a wide range of examples although the discussion of these examples may be incomplete or uneven	Essay uses and discusses some examples although the discussion of these examples may be incomplete or uneven	Essay uses and discusses a limited number of examples and discusses these minimally
Focused and cohesive argument (valid reasoning and organization)	Essay makes a focused and cohesive argument in response to prompt	Essay makes an argument in response to prompt, but the argument may not be fully cohesive or focused throughout	Essay makes an uneven and not particularly clear argument in response to prompt	Essay makes no real argument in response to prompt
Insight and understanding (determines the meaning of and analyzes text)	Essay shows significant insight into and understanding of the text	Essay shows some insight into and understanding of the text	Essay shows limited insight into and understanding of the text	Essay shows little insight into and understanding of the text
Grammar and mechanics (conventions of standard English)	Essay contains few errors in grammar and mechanics, and they do not inhibit meaning; no patterns of error	Essay contains some errors in grammar and mechanics, and they do not inhibit meaning; errors do not fall into patterns	Essay contains frequent errors in grammar and mechanics that may inhibit meaning; writing exhibits some patterns of error	Essay contains numerous errors in grammar and mechanics that inhibit meaning; writing exhibits several patterns of error
Vocabulary use (uses domain-specific vocabulary)	Essay uses precise, varied, and strong vocabulary; several "words to own" from the unit are used correctly	Essay uses some precise, varied, and strong vocabulary; essay attempts to use "words to own" from the unit, but these may be used infrequently or with limited accuracy	Vocabulary choices are sometimes imprecise, repetitive, and weak; essay does not attempt to use "words to own" from the unit or uses these ineffectively and inaccurately	Vocabulary choices are vague, repetitive, and weak; essay does not attempt to use "words to own" from the unit

Category	4—Excellent	3—Good	2—Satisfactory	1—Unsatisfactory
Documentation (in-text citation and works cited)	Essay conforms to the appropriate style guidelines (MLA) for in-text citation and works cited	Essay conforms with limited errors to the appropriate style guidelines (MLA) for in-text citation and works cited	Essay attempts to conform to the appropriate style guidelines (MLA) for in-text citation and works cited but does so ineffectively or inaccurately	Essay does not conform to the appropriate style guidelines (MLA) for in-text citation and works cited
Research (gathers and uses relevant research)	Essay incorporates relevant and appropriate research effectively	Essay displays appropriate research but does not incorporate research fully effectively	Essay displays limited research and incorporates it unevenly	Essays displays little research and incorporates it poorly

About the Authors

Audrey Fisch is a professor of English and the coordinator of secondary English education at New Jersey City University, where she has taught for over twenty years. She has published a wide variety of academic work (including books with Cambridge and Oxford University Presses, numerous scholarly articles, and writing about teaching). She also works as a curriculum consultant and professional development provider for K–12 districts in New Jersey.

Susan Chenelle has taught English and journalism for six years at University Academy Charter High School in Jersey City, New Jersey, where she also has served as the English Department lead and academic director for humanities. She holds a master's degree in education from New Jersey City University and a bachelor's degree in English from Kenyon College. Before becoming a teacher, she was a writer and editor for ten years for publications like MSN.com and Citysearch.com.

Made in the USA
Middletown, DE
03 April 2017